BUSINESS FINANCE DEMYSTIFIED

A GUIDE FOR ENTREPRENEURS, BUSINESS LEADERS, AND TEAMS

ARUL SHANMUGAVELU

Copyright © ARUL SHANMUGAVELU
All Rights Reserved.

This book has been self-published with all reasonable efforts taken to make the material error-free by the author. No part of this book shall be used, reproduced in any manner whatsoever without written permission from the author, except in the case of brief quotations embodied in critical articles and reviews.

The Author of this book is solely responsible and liable for its content including but not limited to the views, representations, descriptions, statements, information, opinions and references ["Content"]. The Content of this book shall not constitute or be construed or deemed to reflect the opinion or expression of the Publisher or Editor. Neither the Publisher nor Editor endorse or approve the Content of this book or guarantee the reliability, accuracy or completeness of the Content published herein and do not make any representations or warranties of any kind, express or implied, including but not limited to the implied warranties of merchantability, fitness for a particular purpose. The Publisher and Editor shall not be liable whatsoever for any errors, omissions, whether such errors or omissions result from negligence, accident, or any other cause or claims for loss or damages of any kind, including without limitation, indirect or consequential loss or damage arising out of use, inability to use, or about the reliability, accuracy or sufficiency of the information contained in this book.

Made with ♥ on the Notion Press Platform
www.notionpress.com

*Dedicated to the leadership of Larsen &
Toubro and the finance professionals who
shaped my understanding of business finance.*

Contents

Foreword

I was delighted to go through Arul's third book, *Business Finance Demystified*, and was struck by its simplicity and forthright style. The book takes a gradual, step-by-step approach, starting from a basic commercial proposition and building up to the Profit & Loss statement, Balance Sheet, and Cash Flow of an enterprise. This progression is an excellent way of introducing readers to the fundamental concepts of corporate finance.

What stood out to me was how the book elegantly links business actions to key return ratios, presenting these concepts in a way that is both insightful and accessible. The sections exploring various facets of business operations, written in an easy-flowing narrative, effectively highlight their connection to value creation. These explanations were truly brilliant and provided readers with a clear understanding of the impact of business decisions on financial performance.

The inclusion of snippet insights and the *Brain Gym* exercises further adds to the book's appeal, offering engaging ways for readers to deepen their understanding. This structure gives the book the feel of being crafted by a teacher of finance, making it an excellent resource for young and aspiring business managers eager to demystify the world of finance.

Business Finance Demystified is a valuable guide for those looking to bridge the gap between functional expertise and financial acumen. It simplifies complex ideas and equips readers with the confidence to navigate the financial dimensions of business with clarity and purpose.

I look forward to seeing more such insightful and impactful books from Arul in the future

R. Shankar Raman
President, Whole-time Director & CFO
Larsen & Toubro Limited

Preface

My journey in the corporate world began as a marketing professional in one of several units of Larsen & Toubro Limited (L&T). I was fortunate to get the opportunity to present our unit's performance to L&T's senior management every quarter. While our unit's Chief Executive was present in such meetings, the Senior Leaders at Corporate headquarters insisted on a younger team member delivering the presentation—a practice aimed at fostering growth and accountability.

Those moments were invaluable.

Standing before the Chairman and CFO in those high-stakes meetings, I quickly realized that the real education wasn't found in textbooks, but in the probing questions that provided insights into our operations, and the unwavering focus on financial health. It was these intense discussions that taught me more about running a business than any MBA program could.

This early exposure became one of my greatest assets when I was eventually appointed Chief Executive of one of Larsen & Toubro's units—a position I held for over a decade. During that time, L&T sold its stake in the unit to Kobe Steel, Inc., Japan. I continued to lead the unit under Japanese management for five years, gaining valuable insights into how a different culture approaches financial management.

Through these experiences, I have come to believe that cost efficiency is the backbone of sustainable success no matter how strong a company's products, services, or innovations may be. Companies often lose sight of this during good times, but once cost control slips, regaining it becomes incredibly difficult. In my opinion, cost efficiency must be ingrained into a company's DNA.

Every person in an organization has the potential to influence the company's financial performance. This book aims to clarify that to every employee and leader, regardless of their department or background. Understanding finance isn't just for accountants—everyone can contribute to cost efficiency and drive the company's success.

Whether you're an entrepreneur, an aspiring leader or someone simply looking to add value to your role, this book offers clear and easy-to-understand insights that make the learning process enjoyable and impactful.

This book is designed to help emerging business leaders grasp the critical role of financial management in building a successful company. It also serves as a practical guide for professionals across various departments, offering insights into how their work directly influences overall business performance."

I hope this book inspires you to explore new ways to contribute, collaborate, and lead with a deeper understanding of the numbers that drive success.

As you turn these pages, may you find not just knowledge, but the confidence to make a significant impact in your professional journey.

Acknowledgements

I am deeply grateful to my Seniors at L&T —Mr. E.S. Kumar, Mr. Vijay Shankar, Mr. N.S. Sivaraman, Mr. S. Venkatraman, Mr. S. Raghavan, and Mr. S.R. Subramanian—whose guidance and insights into business have been invaluable throughout my career. My close interactions with them have greatly enriched my understanding, equipping me with the knowledge and skills necessary to write this book from a business perspective. I was fortunate to work with Mr. K.M. Gopalakrishnan during my initial period, which helped me understand International Trade and Economics, for which I am very thankful.

I also extend my heartfelt thanks to my colleagues in the finance department, Mr. V.N. Somanathan and Mr. G. Muthukrishnan. Years of collaboration with them have given me a deep insight into finance.

A special note of appreciation goes to Mr. Sivaraman, Mr. Krish Venkat, Mr. V.N. Somanathan, Mr. Sivaraj, Mr. Elangovan, and Ms. Priya for their support, encouragement, and willingness to review my manuscript and provide valuable feedback. Their motivation and input have been instrumental in bringing this book to reality.

The Snippets used in this book are created with the help of ChatGPT. I appreciate this tool for its versatility. The rest of the content in this book was created and curated by me.

I thank my professional friend Mr. Unni Krishnan for going through my manuscript and accepting to provide an endorsement to my book. He has been encouraging me from the time I published my first book. His endorsement is printed on the rear cover page.

A Special Thanks

L&T is a very special organisation and I am very fortunate to have worked in it for 3 decades. L&T is an organisation that continuously learns and encourages its employees to learn and apply. We not only learn & hone our professional skills at L&T but also establish a very special bond with the organisation and its people.

I owe what I am to L&T. Hence when I penned this book, I thought it would be a honour if the CFO of L&T could give a Foreword to the book. I was very reluctant to write to him. Would it be fair to ask the CFO of L&T, a diversified corporate mammoth with a revenue of over US$ 25 Bn, for the trivial job of writing a foreword to my book?

Betting on my luck, I sent an email to Mr. Shankar Raman, President, Whole-time Director & CFO of Larsen & Toubro, asking him whether he could write a foreword to my book. I had little hope that he would accept. But, he replied to me *"While I would like to provide the foreword, let me go thro the contents of the book before I confirm."* Amidst his very busy schedule, he was kind enough to go through my book and provide his foreword. This is the love and affection that the senior management of L&T showers on its people. I am eternally thankful to him for fulfilling my dream. Thank you, Sir.

The Prelude to Mastery

CHAPTER ONE

SETTING THE STAGE

"Why Financial Literacy Matters: Setting the Stage for Success"

Understanding finance isn't just a professional skill—it's a life skill. Whether in personal or professional settings, the principles of finance shape the decisions we make and the results we achieve.

In business, every action, regardless of your role or department, influences a company's financial outcomes. Yet, many professionals overlook this connection.

Throughout my four-decade career, I have witnessed capable leaders rise to P&L (Profit & Loss) responsibilities only to struggle due to gaps in financial knowledge.

The consequences of financial illiteracy are not limited to business; they extend to personal life as well. Today, it's common to see young individuals facing financial setbacks due to poor planning and lack of awareness. Interestingly, the principles that govern company finances are remarkably similar to those that govern personal finances—though their importance may differ. Mastering these fundamentals is not just a career advantage; it's a blueprint for financial wellness in all aspects of life.

My attempt in this book is to bring financial literacy to people so that it helps him/ her to run his/ her business. The book also helps individuals to understand how they can grow their careers by contributing to the growth of the organisation.

The book will not attempt anything on how to invest in the stock market or what critical evaluations are required for selecting a company to invest in. However, if someone is not financially literate but would like to start investing in the stock market, then this book would serve to build a strong financial knowledge on which they can build further.

When we talk about a company's performance to a common man he relates it to the profit of the company. Most of the employees feel that a company is evaluated based on its profitability, and hence they look at the Profit & Loss statement to see how much profit is made by the company.

However, 2 other tables need to be reviewed before concluding about the company's status. They are the Balance Sheet and the Cash Flow statement. Many start-ups and entrepreneurs fail to monitor and control these 2 statements thus ending up in a cash crunch or a poor return on their investment and eventually failing in their endeavor though their products or services are successful in the market.

Every action performed by an employee, when translated in money terms affects one or more of these 3 statements viz Profit & Loss Statement, Balance Sheet, and Cashflow statement.

I will demystify these 3 statements in an easy-to-understand manner and explain how these 3 statements affect the business and how individuals can make a positive effect on these statements.

A disclaimer

The statements given in this book are prepared for easier understanding and may not comply with Indian or International accounting standards.

CHAPTER TWO

THE FINANCIAL TRIAD

The three musketeers of business finance - Profit & Loss, Balance Sheet, and Cash Flow.

I refer to the Profit & Loss Statement, Balance Sheet, and Cashflow statement as the Financial Triad, which is a unified force of Business Finance.

To explain this better let us start with a simple example of 3 companies in a car rental business.

Company A owns a Suzuki car at Rs. 1 Mn (Rs. 10 Lakhs)

Company B owns a Honda car at Rs. 2 Mn (Rs. 20 Lakhs)

Company C owns a Benz car at Rs. 5 Mn (Rs. 50 Lakhs)

Each company has a working capital of Rs. 100,000 apart from the investment in the cost of the vehicle.

Company A gets a contract from a company to provide a Car rental service at Rs. 60,000 per month. Similarly, Companies B & C also get a contract at Rs. 80,000 and Rs. 100,000 per month for their Honda and Benz cars respectively.

Let us call this amount the Revenue for the company.

The payment terms for all the 3 contracts are the same, i.e. the payment will be made after 30 days of receiving the invoice. For eg. for the services rendered for March, Company A will raise the invoice on the 1st of April and the payment from the customer is due on 1st of May.

Let's say that the expenses including fuel and driver's salary for a month are Rs. 45,000, Rs. 50,000, and Rs. 60,000 respectively for Companies A, B, and C.

If we make a simple P&L statement, it may look as follows.

Sl	Description	A Suzuki	B Honda	C Benz
1	Revenue for a month	60,000	80,000	100,000
	Revenue for the full year (A)	720,000	960,000	1,200,000
2	Expenses for a month	45,000	55,000	60,000
	Expense for the year	540,000	660,000	720,000
3	Annual Profit (B)	180,000	300,000	480,000
	Profit % (B/A)	25%	31.25%	40%
	Rating based on profitability	3	2	1

Company C made more profits than the others. Can we say that company C is the best among the three?

Pl wait, we need to look at the investment made by these companies, which can be seen in the Balance sheet.

A Balance Sheet shows where the company's money comes from and how it's being used. It lists what the company owns and what it owes, giving a clear view of its financial position. (More details in the forthcoming Chapters)

	Company A	Company B	Company C
Liabilities			
Owner's money	1,100,000	2,100,000	5,100,000
Assets			
Car purchased	1,000,000	2,000,000	5,000,000
Cash for working capital	100,000	100,000	100,000

For the time being, do not worry about the headings Liabilities and Assets. It will be explained later.

From the balance sheet, we may understand the amount invested by the owner in the business, i.e. Rs. 1.1 Mn, 2.1 Mn and 5.1 Mn. Let's calculate the Return on Investment (ROI), i.e. profit earned over the total investment made.

Sl	Description	A	B	C
A	Investment including working capital	1,100,000	2,100,000	5,100,000
B	Annual profit	180,000	300,000	480,000
	Simple Return on Investment B/A	16.4%	14.3%	9.4%
	Rating based on ROI	1	2	3

When we look at the above table we find that Company A made more money for Rs. 100 invested i.e. % of return on the invested amount is more for Company A.

Wow, the scenario has changed !!!

It can now be understood that studying only the P&L is not enough. We need to look at Balance Sheet to see another aspect of the business.

It doesn't end here. We need to see the Cash Flow to check whether these companies will have enough cash to run the business continuously.

You may wonder how a company that makes a profit can go out of cash. Where will the profits go? The answer is that the P&L statement does not show whether the profit is realized or not. Which means, whether the money has come into the company's bank account or not. Or is it only a notional money?

At this point, let's understand that the Revenue mentioned in the P&L shows the value of the products and services that were sold. It does not mention whether this money is received or not.

In the above example, each of the companies started with a cash of Rs. 100,000 as working capital. Their contract with the client was with 30 days credit. This means they will get money from the client only after completion of 30 days of raising the bill. When the companies raise their bill at the end of the first month, it is counted as Revenue earned by the company. But the payment will come only after the end of the second month. So, they will not have any cash inflow from the clients for the first 60 days. The companies should have enough cash to run for 60 days. Let us look at what happens to companies A, B and C.

Sl		Description	A	B	C
	1st month	Cash available with the company at the beginning of the business Opening balance (working capital)	100,000	100,000	100,000
		Revenue	0	0	0
		Expense for 1st 30 days	45,000	55,000	60,000
		Money available at the end of the 30 days	55,000	45,000	40,000
		The companies now raise the invoice on the client. This will be paid after the completion of 30 days, i.e. the receipt of money will come in the first week of the 3rd month only.			
	2nd month	Revenue	0	0	0
		Expenses for second month	45000	55000	60000
		Money available at the end of the second month	10000	-10000 Does not have enough money to complete the 2nd month	-20000 Does not have enough money to complete the 2nd month
	End of 60 days	Rating	1	-	-

Only after the completion of the second month, the money will flow in from the client. However, the company needs to manage till then. In the above case, company A can manage for the first 2 months and can continue to run for the 3rd month, whereas companies B & C can't complete the second month. If they need to complete the second month, they should have an additional amount of Rs. 10000 and Rs. 20000 respectively. In addition, they will need more money to run for about a week in the 3rd month till they receive the money from the client.

I hope the above illustration explains the importance of the Financial Triad.

CHAPTER THREE

BHARAT PENS

Having understood that all the 3 statements are essential for monitoring a business, let us look at a typical manufacturing company. For our study let us call this company Bharat Pens (fictitious). This company is into manufacturing Ball Point Pens. We will review its P&L, Balance Sheet, and Cashflow.

Profit & Loss Statement

Before going into detail, let us understand what constitutes the P&L statement.

P&L is a statement that accumulates

- all revenues that a company received or is due to receive from its customers for the sale of a product or service.
- it also accumulates all the expenses that a company incurred during the financial year for making the sale for that year.

  - These expenses include the cost of raw materials, components, and consumables that the company used in making the products or services that the company sold during the financial year. These expenses should be related to the sales made by the company.

○ The expenses also include the cost of labour, office expenses (electricity, stationary, transport, food, etc), regular maintenance of plant and machinery, taxes and other levies, interest paid to the bank, etc, all related to that year.

It does not include expenses which are paid in advance for services to be availed in the subsequent year.

The revenue and expenses are recognised when the action is performed and not when the actual payment is received or paid.

For eg. When a company make a sale on a credit basis, it will not receive the money when the sale is made, however, the buyer is legally bound to pay the company and hence it is treated as money due to the company and is recognized as revenue.

Similarly, when a company purchases raw materials, or any other items required for the manufacture or sale of goods it may or may not make the payment to the supplier instantly. The company may make the payment in the subsequent months. However, since the company is obligated to pay the supplier, it is recognized as an expense.

The expenses can be classified into Direct Costs and Indirect Costs.

An expense when it is directly consumed in the Sale of goods or services, is recognized as a Direct cost. Let us take the example of Bharat Pens. This company is making ballpoint pens. The Direct expenses for this company will be

1. The plastic raw materials purchased for making the pen.

2. If the plastic raw material is given to the subcontractor for making the outer case of the pen, then the cost of subcontracting the pen on a piece rate is considered a direct cost.
3. The cost of writing ink or the dye filled in the refill
4. The cost of the labour used for making the pens in the plastic moulding machine.
5. The proportionate power used by the machine for each pen, if such a calculation is available.

The above expense should satisfy the following condition.

These expenses should be related to the product that was sold in that year. For eg., if the company purchased Plastics Raw Materials for Rs. 20 Mn and made 2 MN pens, but sold only 1 Mn pens, then it should consider only the proportionate raw material cost, which in this case is Rs. 10 Mn. You might have already paid the full money (Rs. 20 Mn) to the Raw Material supplier. It does not matter; only the cost of raw material related to the sale made is to be considered. The Direct Material costs include the Raw material cost (plastics, sub-contract cost & Dye cost).

We have understood what constitutes Revenue and Direct Material costs. Let us now understand what is Direct labour cost. The Direct labour cost is the cost of labourers who are directly involved in the manufacture of the pens, like the production employees

Let's assume the following

- The price of each pen is Rs. 20
- The company subcontracts some portion of the work and the balance is made in-house.
- The cost of sub-contracting is Rs. 3 per pen.

- The direct labour cost is Rs. 2 per pen.
- Other than the production staff, a company also employs staff in other functions such as HR, Administration, finance, engineering, etc. The company markets the pens through its distributors. Towards this, they incur expenses on Sales staff, transportation cost of the pens to the distributor's warehouse, etc. For simplicity let us group all these expenses under Administrative, Sales, and Distribution expenses and let us say it is Rs. 1 Mn.

No.	Description	Formula	Rs. Mn	Rs. Mn
A	Revenue for 1 Mn pens			20.00
	Cost of Raw material		10.00	
	Cost of Sub Contracting		3.00	
	Cost of Direct labour		2.00	
B	Total Direct Cost			15.00
C	Administrative, Sales and Distribution expenses			1.00
D	Gross Margin	A-B-C		4.00

Now you can see that the company has earned a Gross profit of Rs. 4 Mn. Great. Can they go splashing this out?

Let's think for a moment.

At the time of establishing Bharat Pens, it spent money on buying the land, building the factory, purchasing machinery, etc. Let us assume the company invested as follows.

Land Rs. 10 Mn

Building Rs. 45 Mn

Machinery Rs. 20 Mn

Total Rs. 75 Mn.

The value of these assets changes over a period. The cost of Land normally does not reduce, at least in India. The value of land only increases. Whereas the building becomes old and will be required to be rebuilt after a certain no. of years. Let us assume the building will last for 30 years. It means that the company should have money to rebuild the factory after 30 years in the same place. So, let us recover this amount progressively over 30 years from the profit, i.e. 1/30 every year. This is called depreciation.

Depreciation on account of Building. = 45/30 = i.e 1.5 Mn per year

Similarly, we need to recover the cost of the machinery over its life. The life in number of years needs to be decided by the company based on the type of the machine and its usage. For simplicity let us assume the life of the machine is 10 years.

Depreciation on account of Machinery = 20/10 = Rs. 2 Mn per year

Since the land value will not reduce over time, for accounting we will not consider any depreciation.

However, if the land value had reduced (for some reason) the company can revalue the land and state the same in the P&L and Balance Sheet.

Now, from the Gross margin we need to set aside the amount of Rs. 3.5 Mn (2+1.5) as depreciation.

Gross margin Rs. 4 Mn

Depreciation Rs. 3.5 Mn

Balance Rs. 0.5 Mn

Please note that the amount of Rs. 3.5 Mn (depreciation) is not spent. It is only notional. This is a reserve money for tomorrow's expense.

There is one more point that we forgot.

Did the company borrow any money from the bank or any other party?

Let us assume the company borrowed Rs. 5 Mn from the bank for funding the project and for working capital requirements. The company must pay interest to the lender, is it not? Assuming the interest rate is 5% per annum, the interest amount will work out to Rs. 0.25 Mn. Again remember, it is immaterial whether the company paid this amount at the end of the financial year or not. What is due on 31st March the company may pay in April, but it needs to be recognized as an expense at the end of the year 31st March.

From the balance money let us subtract Rs. 0.25 Mn. Then we arrive at Rs. 0.25 Mn (0.5-0.25).

Is it all over? Wait, one more person is waiting to collect money from the profit that the company has made, i.e. the Government. Yes, Bharat Pens need to pay Taxes to the Government.

Assuming 25% as tax,

Profit before tax = Rs. 0.250 Mn

Tax 25% = Rs. 0.0625 Mn

Profit after Tax = Rs. 0.1875 Mn

Finally, we arrived at the profit of the company which is Rs. 0.1875 Mn i.e. 0.9% of the Sales (0.1875/20)

Let's now consolidate our learning.

No.	Description	Formula	Rs. Mn	Rs. Mn
A	Revenue for 1 Mn pens			20.00
	Cost of Raw material		10.00	
	Cost of Sub Contracting		3.00	
	Cost of Direct labour		2.00	
B	Total Direct Cost			15.00
C	Administrative, Sales and Distribution expenses			1.00
D	Gross Margin	A-B-C		4.00
E	Depreciation			3.50
F	Margin after Depreciation	D-E		0.50
G	Interest payment			0.25
H	Profit before Tax (after Interest payment)	F-G		0.25
I	Tax			0.06
J	Profit after tax	H-I		0.19

Other Income

It is quite normal for a company to receive money from other than direct customers. For example

A company may park the excess cash available from the business for a short period in bank deposits or debt funds. The company might receive a payment of Rs. 10 Mn from a customer but it may not have the requirement of this fund for the next 1 month. It will park this in the bank or mutual fund and earn some interest of say 3 to 5%. This is reported as other income.

Some companies report the following also as other income

- When they do an export, they may receive a duty drawback or export incentive as a percentage of the export sales value. When this is received as Duty Drawback or duty-free licence[1] I would rather prefer this to be reported under material cost. i.e. the cost of materials to be reduced to the extent of the duty drawback received or export incentive received. Because if the export was not there the company would not have received this amount. In the estimation of the product, the company would have factored these benefits to remain competitive. Hence, I feel it should be reflected as a reduction in material cost. For this book, we will retain these as other incomes.

[1] Some countries provide a percentage of the export sales as a licence. This licence can be used for importing material without payment of duty. This benefit is provided by the Government to offset certain disadvantage the country may have.

- Sometimes, the company may also have some non-operative income. For eg., a company owned a car and sold it. This can be figured as extraordinary income. When profit % is computed, we should remove this extraordinary income from the total revenue.

In the above case of the Pen manufacturing company, let us assume they exported 50% of their products and accordingly, they are eligible to get a Duty Drawback (refund of duty). This amount varies depending on the product. For our calculations let's assume it is 1% of the export value.

In addition to this, the government also gives a license (in the form of a scrip). Let's assume this to be another 1% of the export value. This license can be used to import material and pay duty by debiting the licence value. This licence can also be sold in the market for a small reduction in value. For ease of calculation let us assume that the company sells it at a discount of 5% i.e. the company gets 95% value of the licence as cash by selling the licence.

Incidentally, Bharat Pens sold a car that it purchased for its use a few years ago.

Consolidating the other income for Bharat Pens:

- Interest from Bank deposits – let this be Rs. 0.01 Mn
- Duty Drawback – 1% of Rs. 10 Mn export = Rs. 0.1 Mn
- Sale of Duty-free Import licence (scrip) received from the Government

Value of the scrip – 1% of Rs. 10 Mn export = Rs. 0.1 Mn.

This Scrip was sold at a discount of 5%. Hence the company received Rs. 0.095 Mn.

- Sale of car – Bharat Pens sold the car for Rs. 0.5 Mn.

As you can see, the income of the company has increased by Rs. 0.705 Mn. Assuming that there is no increase in the expenses, the profit before tax of the company will go up by Rs. 0.705 Mn.

Profit before tax as per the earlier table = Rs. 0.25 Mn

Additional income as stated above = Rs. 0.705 Mn

Profit before tax = Rs. 0.955 Mn (4.6%)

After paying a tax of 25%, the Profit after tax will be Rs. 0.716 Mn, which is a 3.5% profit.

No.	Description	Formula	Rs. Mn	Rs. Mn
A	Revenue from sale of 1 Mn pens			20.000
	Other Income			0.705
	Interest from Bank Deposit of free cash		0.010	
	Duty draw back from customs	1% of Rs. 10 Mn	0.100	
	Sale of duty free licence scrip @ 1% of exports sold for 5% discount	1% of Rs. 10 Mn * 0.95	0.095	
	Sale of assets (car)		0.500	
	Total Revenue			20.705
	Cost of Raw material		10.000	
	Cost of Sub Contracting		3.000	
	Cost of Direct labour		2.000	
B	Total Direct Cost			15.000
C	Administrative, Sales and Distribution expenses			1.000
D	Gross Margin	A-B-C		4.705
E	Depreciation			3.500
F	Margin after Depreciation	D-E		1.205
G	Interest payment			0.250
H	Profit before Tax (after Interest payment)	F-G		0.955
I	Tax			0.239
J	Profit after tax	H-I		0.716

Kindly note that other income due to the sale of some assets is normally removed from the total revenue while calculating the profitability of the company, since this income is not due to the normal business operations. Hence the PBT from the business operation is Rs. 955 Mn - Rs. 0.5 Mn = Rs. 0.455 Mn.

<u>Snippet - 1</u>

*In the years before the 20th century, what we now call the **Profit & Loss statement** was often known as the Trading and Profit & Loss Account or simply the Profit & Loss Account. Some organizations referred to it as the Income and Expenditure Statement, particularly for non-commercial purposes. Back then, financial statements were not as standardized as today. Companies commonly separated their records into a Trading Account, covering revenues and direct costs, and a Profit & Loss Account for overheads and other operational expenses. Over time, this evolved into today's consolidated Income Statement format, capturing a business's overall financial performance in one place.*

Balance Sheet

While the Profit & Loss statement indicates the total revenue & expenses for the whole financial year, the balance sheet indicates the company's assets and liabilities at a given point in time, called the reporting date. This is normally reported as of the end of the financial year. People refer to this statement as a photo shoot on the last day (in the financial year) of the operations of the company. So, this statement reflects what is owned & owed by the company on a particular day.

What is owned by the company includes land, buildings, machinery, materials lying in the store, cash in the bank, and payment that is receivable from the customers.

What is owed by the company includes the money that the owners have given to the company, the retained earnings, what is borrowed from the bank and what is required to be paid to the vendors.

Now let us try to build a balance sheet for this company. As mentioned earlier, the company spent Rs. 75 Mn for purchasing the land, building the factory and purchasing the machines. Let's assume that the owners of the company had given Rs 65 Mn as their equity and the company through its business had earned in the past years some profits. Out of this profit, a portion was given to the owners in the form of Dividends and the balance is retained by the company for its future use, which is called retained earnings. Let's assume it is Rs. 5.7 Mn. To cater to the day-to-day expenses, the company borrowed Rs 5 Mn from the bank as a working capital loan, for which it is paying interest. We have accounted for this interest as an expense in the Profit & Loss statement.

The above explanation may be tabulated as follows.

Balance Sheet		
	Particulars	Rs. Mn
Liabilities		
	Equity	65.0
	Retained earnings	5.7
	Borrowings	5.0
	vendor payables	1.0
		76.7
Assets		
	Land	10.0
	Building	43.5
	Plant and Machinery	18.0
	Inventory	4.0
	Receivables from stockist	1.0
	Cash in Bank	0.2
		76.7

The investment from the owners is the Equity and the retained earnings, i.e. Rs. 70.7 Mn. The return on investment is

profit before tax (Rs. 0.95 Mn) / Investment (Rs. 70.7 Mn) = 1.3%

This is a poor return on investment. It means that the profit earned for the invested money is very low. Bharat pens have a clear work cut out for them, i.e. improving the Return on Investment.

<u>Snippet 2</u>

*The **balance sheet** concept dates back to the Italian Renaissance, where merchants needed to track their assets and debts. Inspired by Pacioli's double-entry bookkeeping, they used "debito" (debt) and "credito" (credit) as core concepts. The left side, or "debit," represented assets, things owned, and the right side, or "credit," represented liabilities or what was owed to others. This system allowed merchants to visually "balance" their wealth and obligations, and it became the backbone of the balance sheet format we know today.*

Nowadays companies may not show the assets and liabilities in the left and right side of the same table. It is given one below the other. Some companies mention assets on the top and some others mention it in the bottom.

Cashflow Statement

At the end of the year, we should calculate whether the company has generated cash or not. As discussed in the earlier chapters the mere profit shown in the Profit & Loss statement does not mean we have that cash in our hand. To check whether the company has generated cash we need to consider the following

The cash profit the company has made for the given year and the difference in the inventory, payables, receivables, and cash compared to the previous year. Without complicating much we will stay only with this understanding for generating the cash statement. Let us assume the numbers for inventory, receivables, payables, and cash in hand are as follows for the Current Year and the Previous Year.

Details from Balance Sheet	Previous Year	Current Year		Difference
Liabilities	Rs. Mn	Rs. Mn		Rs. Mn
vendor payables	1.5	1.0		-0.5
Assets				
Invetory	4.1	4.0		0.1
Receivables	1.9	1.0		0.9
Cash in Hand	0.2	0.2		0.0
Total				0.5

You may observe the following from the above table.

1. The vendor payable at Rs 1.5 Mn in the previous year is now reduced to Rs. 1 Mn, which means the cash generated from the operations during the current year has been used to clear the outstanding to the extent of Rs. 0.5 Mn.

2. The inventory has reduced by 0.1 Mn releasing that much cash into the business.
3. The collections that were due from the stockist at Rs. 1.9 Mn is now reduced to Rs. 1 Mn thus releasing the cash of 0.9 Mn to the business.
4. There is no change in Cash in Hand.

The reductions in points 2 & 3 are the direct release of locked-up working capital in the business. In the above example, the amount of cash released from the locked-up working capital is Rs. 1 Mn (0.1+0.9).

At the same time, you would see that the company was holding vendors' money to the tune of Rs. 1.5 Mn at the end of the previous year which is now reduced to Rs. 1 Mn which means an additional Rs. 0.5 million is used for clearing the dues of the vendors.

So, from the above table (change in working capital), we can understand that there is an increase in cash flow to the extent of Rs. 1 Mn and there is a reduction in cash flow to the extent of Rs. 0.5 Mn and hence the net increase in cash is Rs. 0.5 Mn.

Now going back to the Profit & Loss statement, the profit the company gained before tax payment was Rs. 0.95 Mn. The depreciation of Rs. 3.5 Mn is not an expense but a provision. So the total cash generated by the company is as follows

Profit before tax = Rs. 0.95 Mn

Depreciation = Rs. 3.50 Mn

From the above table (change in working capital) = Rs. 0.50 Mn

Total Cash generated = Rs. 4.95 Mn

Setting aside the tax to be paid (i.e. Rs. 0.24 Mn) the net cash useable by the company is Rs. 4.71 Mn.

Snippet 3

__Depreciation__ may seem like a modern accounting concept, but it actually has roots in Ancient Rome. Roman accountants had to keep track of the wear and tear on warships, knowing that these ships lost value with each voyage. To address this, they began adjusting the value of these assets over time, ensuring they knew the true worth of their fleet at any given moment. This was an early form of depreciation, acknowledging that assets lose value as they're used—a practice that's now essential in financial reporting.

Future Cashflow for the Bharat Pens

What we saw in the earlier paragraphs is a postmortem, i.e. what has already happened. To ensure that companies do not run out of cash at any point, the Leadership team of the company look at future cashflows during their review. They review the potential cash flow for the next 1 to 2 years to ensure they do not run out of cash at any time. Such a statement for Bharat Pens is shown in the next page.

The inflow represents the cash to be received from customers/stockists and also other income such as Duty drawback, sale of duty-free import licence, interest from deposits etc.

The outflow represents payment to be made to vendors, employees, statutory bodies, etc.

The closing balance should be a positive number indicating that the company has cash after meeting the cash requirements for the month.

In case this number is negative then we should take some action such as postponing some expenses, reducing some expenses, etc. to ensure that the closing balance is positive. In case this is not possible then the company may have to resort to borrowings from the bank.

From the table on the next page, you can understand that Bharat Pens has a healthy Cash Flow.

The opening balance indicated in the table is the closing balance of the Previous Year. Let's assume it to be Rs. 0.2 Mn.

Further, the following assumptions are made to prepare the cash flow statement for Bharat Pens.

The Total customer collection for the year is the same as the Sales Revenue of the company and it is collected equally in all 12 months.

Similarly, the expenses such as Vendor payment. Salary & wages and other expenses are made equally in 12 months.

Inflow Rs. Mn	Apr	May	Jun	Jul	Aug	Sep	Oct	Nov	Dec	Jan	Feb	Mar	Total
Opening balance	0.20	0.56	0.88	1.19	1.55	1.87	2.68	2.80	3.12	3.43	3.79	4.10	
Customer collection	1.67	1.67	1.67	1.67	1.67	1.67	1.67	1.67	1.67	1.67	1.67	1.67	20.00
Other income	0.05			0.05		0.50	0.05			0.05			0.71
Outflow													
Vendor payment	1.08	1.08	1.08	1.08	1.08	1.08	1.08	1.08	1.08	1.08	1.08	1.08	13.00
salary and wages	0.17	0.17	0.17	0.17	0.17	0.17	0.17	0.17	0.17	0.17	0.17	0.17	2.00
Other expenses	0.08	0.08	0.08	0.08	0.08	0.08	0.08	0.08	0.08	0.08	0.08	0.08	1.00
interest payment WC loan	0.02	0.02	0.02	0.02	0.02	0.02	0.02	0.02	0.02	0.02	0.02	0.02	0.25
Tax							0.24						0.24
Closing balance	0.56	0.88	1.19	1.55	1.87	2.68	2.80	3.12	3.43	3.79	4.10	4.42	

Cash Flow Statement of Bharat Pens

Brain Gym - I

1. Prepare a P&L statement for Bharat pens considering that it sold 1.5 Mn pens instead of 1 Mn pens. (Assume that the direct costs will be proportional to the number of pens sold.) The Administrative, Sales and Distribution expenses went up by 10% from the Rs. 1 Mn. The exports for the year was Rs. 15 Mn, and the interest from deposits was Rs. 0.1 Mn. There were no sales of any assets.

2. For the above scenario, calculate the PBT Margin and Return on Investment.

The Core Insight

CHAPTER FOUR

ABC LIMITED

The purpose of this book is twofold. First, it provides a clear guideline for entrepreneurs & individuals stepping into the role of Profit & Loss (P&L) responsibility for the first time, helping them understand and manage the key financial levers that drive business success. Second, it helps professionals across various departments to have a deeper understanding of how their specific roles can positively impact the company's overall performance. By linking day-to-day actions with broader financial outcomes, the book bridges the gap between departmental work and company-wide success.

Each department in a company whether it is marketing, production, purchase, human resources, administration, finance, plant engineering, IT, etc. can make a profound impact on the financial performance of the company. Collectively it will make a big impact on the company's performance. The job of the CEO is to ensure that his team is aware of their potential and motivate them to contribute towards improving the financials.

In the forthcoming chapters, we will see how each of the departments or functions of an organization can impact the performance of the company.

For this purpose, I have tabulated a P&L statement, Balance Sheet and cash flow sheet of a hypothetical company called ABC Limited. Let us consider this to be an engineering company making a product to sell into a B-to-B segment.

ABC Limited has a Sales of Rs. 26,500 Mn with a gross margin of Rs 2,812 Mn. The company made a profit of Rs 2,041 Mn before taxes. The profit after tax stood at Rs. 1,531 Mn.

Please refer to the table below for further understanding.

Profit / Loss Statement

	Profit & Loss			
No.	Description	Formula	Rs. Mn	% on sales
A	Revenue from operations		26,500	
B	Direct Material cost		19,978	75.4%
C	Employee Benefit		1,345	5.1%
D	Manufacturing expense		1,836	6.9%
E	Sales & Admin expense		529	2.0%
F	Gross Margin	A-B-C-D-E	2,812	10.6%
G	Depreciation		631	
H	Margin after Depreciation	F-G	2,181	
I	Interest payment		140	
J	Profit Before Tax (PBT)	H-I	2,041	7.7%
K	Tax		510	
L	Profit after tax (PAT)	J-K	1,531	5.8%

Kindly note the following

- The cost of material consumed is 75.4%
- The cost of employee benefits is 5.1%
- The Manufacturing expense is 6.9%
- The Sales & Admin expense is 2%
- The Gross margin is 10.6%

- The PBT % is 7.7%
- The PAT % is 5.8%

The above percentages are calculated on the total revenue of the company.

As you can see this is a business with high material costs and relatively a small value addition by the company. Critical parts are made in-house in their manufacturing shop. Since the company operates in a B2B segment the sales expenses are lower. Generally, in the case of the B2C segment, the marketing costs are higher.

Balance Sheet

ABC Limited is an old company that was started with an equity investment of Rs. 348 Mn. Over the years the company earned profit and paid part of it as a dividend and retained the balance for its use, which works out to Rs. 3508 Mn. Now the total of Rs. 3856 Mn belongs to the owners of the company hence it is a liability to the company.

To fund expansion the company has borrowed Rs. 1211 Mn. This will be repaid over a few years. Together with other long-term liabilities the total long-term (Non-current) liabilities stand at Rs. 1936 Mn.

To fund the day-to-day operations of paying vendors, employee salary, etc the company has a short-term borrowing of Rs. 1,033 Mn.

The company owes Rs. 4,130 Mn to the vendors, for the materials purchased on a credit basis.

Other current liabilities stand at Rs. 845 Mn. This could be some advances received from customers or dealers, statutory payments yet to be made, etc.

The total of the current liabilities stands at Rs. 6,008 Mn.

The total of the liabilities (Non-current & current) is Rs. 11,800 Mn.

Generally, the company is evaluated based on the Profit earned by One share. In the case of ABC Limited the equity is Rs. 348 Mn.

Let's assume that the face value of the share is Rs. 10. This means the number of shares is 34.8 Mn. This 34.8 Mn share has earned a profit of Rs. 1,531 Mn. Each share has earned 1531/34.8 = Rs. 43.99 per share. This is known as Earnings Per Share (EPS).

Apart from the equity, there could be other borrowings. The company can borrow from the bank, the owners, or from other financial institutions. The company puts this money into the purchase of assets and other investments.

No	Description	Rs. Mn	Rs. Mn
a	Equity Share capital		348.0
b	Reserves and Surplus		3,508.0
A	Total shareholders funds	a+b	3,856.0
c	Long term borrowings		1,211.0
d	Other liabilities and long term provisions		725.0
B	Total non current liabilities	c+d	1,936.0
e	Short term borrowings		1,033.0
f	Trade payables		4,130.0
g	Other current liabilities and provision		845.0
C	Total current liabilities	e+f+g	6,008.0
	Grand total of liabilities	A+B+C	**11,800.0**
	Assets		
h	Tangible assets		6,260.0
i	Intangible asset		688.0
j	Capital WIP		574.0
k	Other financial assets		611.0
D	Total non current asset	h+i+j+k	8,133.0
m	Current investments		191.0
n	Inventories		1,236.0
o	Trade receivables		955.0
p	Cash and cash equivalents		242.0
q	Other current assets		1,043.0
E	Total current assets	m+n+o+p+q	3,667.0
	Grand total of the asset	D+E	11,800.0

Balance Sheet

From the table given above, we can understand how this money has been utilized by this company.

The company could receive advances from its clients, dealers, or stockists. These are current liabilities and will normally used to fund the current assets (inventory). The credit extended by the Suppliers/ Vendors is useful to the Company to manage their cashflow requirements.

At this juncture, I would like to explain the concept of a legal entity. A company is like an individual (a person). The company is separate from the owners (collectively referred to as shareholders) who created it. Hence it is treated as an entity different from the owners. So, whatever money the owners give to the company is treated as an equity or loan. Hence this amount is considered as a liability for the company and it should return this money to the owner (like an individual who has borrowed) wants it.

For the amount taken as a loan from the owners or from the bank the company needs to pay interest to the owners or to the bank, irrespective of whether the company makes profit or not.

However, for the money received from the owners as equity the company will pay back in the form of dividend, only if it makes profit. Out of the profits earned by the company, typically, the company keeps the money for its expansion and running of the business and pays the balance amount to the owners in the form of dividend. The money that is kept by the company for its future use is called the accumulated profits or retained earnings.

With the above money (Rs. 11,800 Mn), the company has purchased tangible assets for Rs 6,260 million and intangible assets such as technology, software, etc., for Rs 688 million. Rs 574 million has been spent on the procurement of machines and buildings which are yet to be completed/commissioned.

The other financial assets of Rs. 611 Mn under the non-current category refer to long-term loans extended by the company to other companies, long-term advances, investments in other companies, etc.

The company has invested the idle funds of Rs. 191 Mn on short-term deposits, classified as current investments. The value of the inventory available in the company is Rs 1,236 Mn. The company has to receive Rs 955 Mn from its customers or dealers. Rs 242 Mn is in the form of cash in the bank account. This gives the complete account of how Rs 11,800 Mn is utilized by the company.

Snippet-4

Normally we value only physical assets, later came the intangible asset like software which we can not see physically. There is one more category of asset called Goodwill.

***Goodwill**, an asset on the balance sheet, has origins in the 19th century when companies began valuing intangible qualities. When one business bought another, they noticed that factors like a strong reputation, loyal customer base, or brand value contributed to its worth but weren't physical assets. Accountants labeled this value as "goodwill," reflecting the positive sentiment and established relationships that added to a company's worth. Today, goodwill remains a significant part of many acquisition valuations, representing that "extra" worth beyond tangible assets.*

Cashflow

Kindly refer to the cash flow statement. As mentioned earlier, this is one of the 3 most important financial tables for a business. This tabulates the cash that would come into the company from the customers when they pay for Goods and Services and any borrowings that the company may receive from the Bank.

The company is required to manage its outflow based on this incoming cash, for paying to the Vendors, employees, statutory bodies, loan repayment, interest, etc. From the table, you will find that the closing balance at the end of the month varies from a negative Rs 122 Mn to a positive Rs. 829 Mn. A negative balance signifies that there is a shortage of money to meet the cash outflows for the month. Hence something needs to be done.

The cash balance for September is – Rs. 116 Mn. To avoid this situation the company could reduce the expenses in September or earlier. Alternatively, it can postpone some outflows from September to the month when there is surplus cash. For our discussion let us assume that we cannot reduce the expense. So we should find some way to shift some payments that are due in September to October or November. I have selected to shift the capital expenses in such a way that the closing balance remains positive. The modified cells are shown in grey and bold letters. The total expense for the year for the capital account remains at Rs. 1000 Mn.

Inflow Rs. Mn	Apr	May	Jun	Jul	Aug	Sep	Oct	Nov	Dec	Jan	Feb	Mar
Opening balance	242	464	687	682	706	829	-116	8	133	-47	-122	103
Customer collection	2208	2208	2208	2208	2208	2208	2208	2208	2208	2208	2208	2208
working capital loan												
Outflow												
Vendor payment	1665	1665	1665	1665	1665	1665	1665	1665	1665	1665	1665	1665
salary and wages	112	112	112	112	112	112	112	112	112	112	112	112
Manufacturing expenses	153	153	153	153	153	153	153	153	153	153	153	153
Sales & Admin expenses	44	44	44	44	44	44	44	44	44	44	44	44
interest payment LT loan	6	6	6	6	6	6	6	6	6	6	6	6
interest payment WC loan	6	6	6	5	5	5	4	4	4	3	3	3
loan repayment			150			150			150			150
Statutory payment - Tax			77			154			154			128
Dividends						765						
capital investment				200	100	100	100	100	100	300		
Closing balance	464	687	682	706	829	-116	8	133	-47	-122	103	50

Alternatively, the company could take an overdraft from the bank for the months where there is negative cash flow and repay it in the months where there is positive cash flow. When we take overdraft there will be a requirement to pay interest on the overdraft which needs to be paid in the subsequent month, which is factored in the interest payment.

Option 1 - Deferring some expenses

Inflow Rs. Mn	Apr	May	Jun	Jul	Aug	Sep	Oct	Nov	Dec	Jan	Feb	Mar
Opening balance	242	464	687	682	706	849	4	8	133	3	8	103
Customer collection	2208	2208	2208	2208	2208	2208	2208	2208	2208	2208	2208	2208
working capital loan	0	0	0	0	0	0	0	0	0	0	0	0
Outflow												
Vendor payment	1665	1665	1665	1665	1665	1665	1665	1665	1665	1665	1665	1665
salary and wages	112	112	112	112	112	112	112	112	112	112	112	112
Manufacturing expenses	153	153	153	153	153	153	153	153	153	153	153	153
Sales & Admin expenses	44	44	44	44	44	44	44	44	44	44	44	44
interest payment LT loan	6	6	6	6	6	6	6	6	6	6	6	6
interest payment WC loan	6	6	6	5	5	5	4	4	4	3	3	3
loan repayment	0	0	150	0	0	150	0	0	150	0	0	150
Statutory payment – Tax	0	0	77	0	0	154	0	0	154	0	0	128
Dividends	0	0	0	0	0	765	0	0	0	0	0	0
capital investment	0	0	0	200	80	0	220	100	50	220	130	
Closing balance	464	687	682	706	849	4	8	133	3	8	103	50

Option 2 - Borrowing - overdraft

Inflow Rs. Mn	Apr	May	Jun	Jul	Aug	Sep	Oct	Nov	Dec	Jan	Feb	Mar
Opening balance	242	464	687	682	706	829	4	128	131	2	7	103
Customer collection	2208	2208	2208	2208	2208	2208	2208	2208	2208	2208	2208	2208
working capital loan	0	0	0	0	0	120	0	0	50	80	0	0
Outflow												
Vendor payment	1665	1665	1665	1665	1665	1665	1665	1665	1665	1665	1665	1665
salary and wages	112	112	112	112	112	112	112	112	112	112	112	112
Manufacturing expenses	153	153	153	153	153	153	153	153	153	153	153	153
Sales & Admin expenses	44	44	44	44	44	44	44	44	44	44	44	44
interest payment LT loan	6	6	6	6	6	6	6	6	6	6	6	6
interest payment WC loan	6	6	6	5	5	5	5	5	4	4	4	3
loan repayment	0	0	150	0	0	150	0	120	150	0	130	150
Statutory payment – Tax	0	0	77	0	0	154	0	0	154	0	0	128
Dividends	0	0	0	0	0	765	0	0	0	0	0	0
capital investment	0	0	0	200	100	100	100	100	100	300	0	0
Closing balance	464	687	682	706	829	4	128	131	2	7	101	50

Cashflow Statements

Snippet 5

*The **cash flow statement** as we know it wasn't standard in financial reporting until the 1980s. Before then, many companies focused mainly on the income statement and balance sheet. However, during the economic struggles of the 1970s, analysts noticed that some companies looked profitable on paper but were struggling with cash—many even went bankrupt. Investors and managers realized they needed a clearer view of how cash was moving through a business. In 1987, the Financial Accounting Standards Board (FASB) made the cash flow statement a required part of financial reporting in the U.S., adding an extra layer of clarity on liquidity and solvency.*

If you have understood these tables well, we can proceed to understand how each function of a company will impact the financials of a company.

This book can serve as a guide for any person seeking a leadership role in a company and for individuals who want to excel in their functional area by bringing out their best.

CHAPTER FIVE

SUPPLY CHAIN

"The silent orchestrator that ensures the right things arrive at the right time, driving efficiency and trust."

Ram is the head of the Supply Chain function at ABC Limited. He has over 20 years of experience in Supply Chain function. There are 10 people in his team. Each of them focuses on specific areas of purchasing such as raw materials, components, consumables, inventory, etc., required for the manufacture of the end product. The team is also responsible for the purchase of capital assets and inventory management.

Vishal is the new President appointed by the Board of Directors to head ABC Limited. He comes with a strong background in finance. During the introductory meeting with Ram, he urged Ram to show financial improvements in his area of work. Ram argued that he has been handling Supply Chain for many years at ABC and it is already at its optimum. Vishal told him, Ram, I can understand your confidence in your job, and I appreciate the same. However, there is always some scope for improvement. I'm not asking for any big reduction in cost or a big increase in the credit.

Just minor improvements in Material cost, Inventory, Vendor credit, capital cost reduction, etc. Ram, I can assure you that I am not going to push you continuously on this. Let us see what is possible. Please do it with passion and not as a target to reach. I am not keeping any target. Don't worry.

With this brief Ram started to think about what he could do in those areas.

(Since this book is not about how to conduct a Supply Chain function I will not be dwelling on the methods of cost reduction or inventory reduction. I will be focusing on how this will have an impact on the financials of the company.)

Material Cost

Ram called his team of buyers and asked them to list down the items that they procured. The total amount of purchases for a year was Rs. 19978 Mn. The typical approach is an 80:20 analysis. The team listed the 20% of the material that constitutes 80% of the cost and Ram asked his team to work scientifically to identify the potential cost reduction possibilities. A target of 5% was kept. This is a very big target considering that the company has matured itself in procurement over the years.

The team looked at various possibilities such as alternate vendors, alternate processes of manufacture, new technology alternatives, combining certain activities, reducing freight by combining purchases, annual contracts for repeated items, etc. They were able to get a 5% reduction only in a few of the components. At the end of the exercise, they achieved a reduction of just 1% on the total value.

Ram reported this to Vishal. Vishal congratulated Ram and went on to explain the following.

Ram, the reduction that you achieved will positively hit the bottom line. 1% translates into Rs. 200 Mn (1% of Rs. 19978 Mn). This will directly increase the PBT by Rs. 200 Mn. i.e. the PBT will increase from Rs. 2041 Mn to Rs. 2241 Mn, almost a 10% jump in the profit.

Vishal explained this to Ram with the following table.

The materials cost which stood at Rs 19,978 Mn was reduced to Rs 19,778 Mn thus providing a reduction in the material cost of Rs 200 Mn. This reduction in material cost will positively impact the Profit before tax. The table below shows the P&L before the material cost reduction and after the material cost reduction.

You may also observe that the EPS has also increased due to the above reduction. This increase in EPS has a direct positive impact on the share price.

No.	Description	Formula	Rs. Mn		Scenario 1
					Material Cost reduction
A	Revenue from operations		26,500		26,500.0
B	Direct Material cost		19,978		19,778.2
C	Employee Benefit		1,345		1,345.0
D	Manufacturing expense		1,836		1,836.0
E	Sales & Admin expense		529		529.0
F	Gross Margin	A-B-C-D-E	2,812		3,011.8
G	Depreciation		631		631.0
H	Margin after Depreciation	F-G	2,181		2,380.8
I	Interest payment		140		140.0
J	Profit before Tax (after Interest payment)	H-I	2,041		2,240.8
K	Tax		510		560.2
L	Profit after tax	J-K	1,531	7%	1,680.6
	Earnings per Share		43.99		48.29

Ram was thrilled that his effort pushed the profit by 10%.

Ram and his team were motivated by seeing the potential benefit that the company could achieve by the above exercise. Fueled by this success, the team started to explore other areas such as inventory and credit terms with their Vendors.

Credit Terms

The team looked at various vendor categories and their respective credit terms. The credit terms were between 30 to 60 days in most of the cases. The team spoke to the major Vendors to see whether the terms could be extended by 15 to 30 days without causing major discomfort to the vendors. The team convinced a few vendors who were willing to move from 30 to 45 days or to 60 days.

There were a few vendors to whom the company was paying a down payment (also known as Advance) of 20% at the time of placement of Purchase Orders. On discussing with them, some of the vendors agreed to accept the Purchase Orders without any down payment. A few of them agreed to reduce the amount of down payment to 10% or 15%. The net effect of all these changes resulted in an increase of 2 days in the weighted average credit.

How to calculate the weighted average of credit in "number of days"? Kindly refer to the insert at the end of this chapter.

Now let us look at how this is going to benefit the company. From the Profit & Loss statement, we can see that the total materials purchased by the company is Rs 19,978 Mn. The weighted average credit extension was 2 days. As you know the company has borrowed short-term funds to manage its operation. When we get additional credit from the vendors, to that extent the company can delay taking the working capital loan or repay what it has taken already. A simple calculation of 2 days' interest upon the total material cost works out to Rs. 10.9 million at the rate of 10% per annum.

The annual total purchases = Rs. 19978 Mn

Purchase per day = Rs. 19978/365= Rs. 54.7 Mn

Credit extension of 2 days means = 54.7 X 2 = Rs. 109.4 Mn

Rs 109.4 Mn is reduced from the payment to be made to vendors. Interest at the rate of 10% pa will work out to Rs. 10.9 Mn

The table below shows the P&L wherein you can observe that the interest cost has come down to Rs. 129 Mn instead of 140 Mn, resulting in an increase in Profit (PAT) by about Rs. 8 Mn

You may observe that the EPS has marginally improved from Rs. 43.99 to Rs. 44.22. You may ask, is it significant? Please note that we have increased the credit just by 2 days. If we can increase by a substantial period then the effect will be significant.

No.	Description	Formula	Rs. Mn		Scenario 2
					credit terms with Vendors
A	Revenue from operations		26,500		26,500.0
B	Direct Material cost		19,978		19,978.0
C	Employee Benefit		1,345		1,345.0
D	Manufacturing expense		1,836		1,836.0
E	Sales & Admin expense		529		529.0
F	Gross Margin	A-B-C-D-E	2,812		2,812.0
G	Depreciation		631		631.0
H	Margin after Depreciation	F-G	2,181		2,181.0
I	Interest payment		140		129.1
J	Profit before Tax (after Interest payment)	H-I	2,041		2,051.9
K	Tax		510		513.0
L	Profit after tax	J-K	1,531	6%	1,539.0
	Earnings per Share		43.99		44.22

<u>Snippet - 6</u>

India's contributions *to financial accounting are significant, with roots in ancient practices, traditional systems, and modern adaptations. India has one of the oldest recorded histories of financial and administrative systems.*
Arthashastra (4th Century BCE)*, authored by Chanakya (Kautilya), is one of the earliest texts on economics, governance, and accounting.*

Inventory reduction

The team's focus shifted to Inventory management.

The inventory at the end of the year stood at Rs 1236 Mn. For ease of our calculation let us assume this is the average inventory throughout the year. i.e. the inventory at the end of each day was Rs. 1236 Mn. Ram and his team worked very closely with the planning and production departments to identify how they could cut down inventory without affecting production. By educating the vendors on OTD (On-time Delivery) and helping them to establish a robust manufacturing process they embarked on a program for reducing the inventory by about 10%. Specific items were identified and their reorder levels were reduced. Over time, Ram's team was able to achieve an inventory reduction of 10%.

Let's look at what impact it had on the financials.

As mentioned, the impact of the 10% reduction in Inventory on the Balance Sheet and P&L would take a long time since the existing excess inventory should get consumed first. However, for our calculations let's assume that the impact of inventory reduction has already taken effect.

With a 10% reduction in Inventory, the reduction will be Rs. 123.6 Mn. This means the borrowing of the company can be reduced to the same amount. Hence the interest burden will come down by Rs. 12.36 Mn when worked out at 10% per annum.

This will increase the profit by Rs. 12.4 Mn at the PBT level and Rs. 9 Mn at the PAT level.

The EPS will improve from Rs. 43.99 to Rs. 44.25.

No.	Description	Formula	Rs. Mn		Scenario 3
					reduction in Inventory
A	Revenue from operations		26,500		26,500.0
B	Direct Material cost		19,978		19,978.0
C	Employee Benefit		1,345		1,345.0
D	Manufacturing expense		1,836		1,836.0
E	Sales & Admin expense		529		529.0
F	Gross Margin	A-B-C-D-E	2,812		2,812.0
G	Depreciation		631		631.0
H	Margin after Depreciation	F-G	2,181		2,181.0
I	Interest payment		140		127.6
J	Profit before Tax (after Interest payment)	H-I	2,041		2,053.4
K	Tax		510		513.3
L	Profit after tax	J-K	1,531	6%	1,540.0
	Earnings per Share		43.99		44.25

ROCE and ROE

Apart from EPS, the Return on Capital Employed (ROCE) & Return on Equity (ROE) are important measures.

ROCE is the % of earnings made on the capital employed and the ROE is the % of earnings on the equity & retained earnings (owners' money)

The capital employed is of the total Equity (including retained earnings) and long-term borrowings, i.e. Rs. 3856 Mn & Rs. 1936 Mn = Rs. 5792 Mn (Denominator). The Numerator is the income before Interest and Tax (PBIT)*.

Using the owner's money and the money borrowed from bankers the company has earned PBIT. So this is the Numerator. In our case, the PBIT is Rs. 2181 Mn. The ROCE is (Rs. 2181 Mn/ Rs. 5792 Mn) * 100 = 37.66%

The ROE has the PAT as the numerator and Equity (including retained earnings) as the denominator. i.e (Rs. 1531/ Rs. 3856) * 100 = 39.70 %

Balance Sheet			
No	Description	Rs. Mn	Rs. Mn
a	Equity Share capital		348.0
b	Reserves and Surplus		3,508.0
A	Total shareholders funds	a+b	3,856.0
c	Long term borrowings		1,211.0
d	Other liabilities and long term provisions		725.0
B	Total non current liabilities	c+d	1,936.0

(*For simplicity I am following the above formula. The appropriate way of doing it is by calculating NOPAT (Net operating profit after Tax). i.e. PAT + Intertest. I am not going to use this as it may confuse the readers.)

Vendor Credit – Weighted Average

Let's assume that the purchase by the company for the full year is Rs. 10000 Mn. This purchase is done with differing payment terms. Two scenarios are portrayed below for better understanding. You may find that the vendor credit on the weighted average basis has improved from 41 days to 44 days.

Total material cost Rs. Mn (for full year)		10000	
The Initial Scenario			
	credit days	Purchase value Rs. Mn	Proportionate credit days on total purchase
value of purchases with 60 days credit	60	5000	30
value of purchases with 30 days credit	30	3000	9
value of purchases with immediate payment (no credit)	0	1000	0
Value of purchases with advance payment of 20% and balance 30 days after material receipt		1000	
20% advance (paid 90 days before material arrival date)	-90	200	-2
balance 80% paid after 30 days	45	800	4
Total credit days enjoyed by the company			41
The Revised Scenario			
	credit days	Purchase value Rs. Mn	Proportionate credit days on total purchase
value of purchases with 60 days credit	60	5500	33
value of purchases with 30 days credit	30	3000	9
value of purchases with immediate payment (no credit)	0	500	0
Value of purchases with advance payment of 20% and balance 30 days after material receipt		1000	
20% advance (paid 90 days before material arrival date)	-90	200	-2
balance 80% paid after 30 days	45	800	4
Total credit days enjoyed by the company			44

Brain GYM – II

1. For the 3 scenarios shown in the earlier pages, calculate the ROCE and ROE.
2. Assuming that all 3 scenarios are implemented simultaneously, what will be the combined effect on P&L?

CHAPTER SIX

MARKETING

"The storyteller of your business—building the bridge between your product and the people it serves."

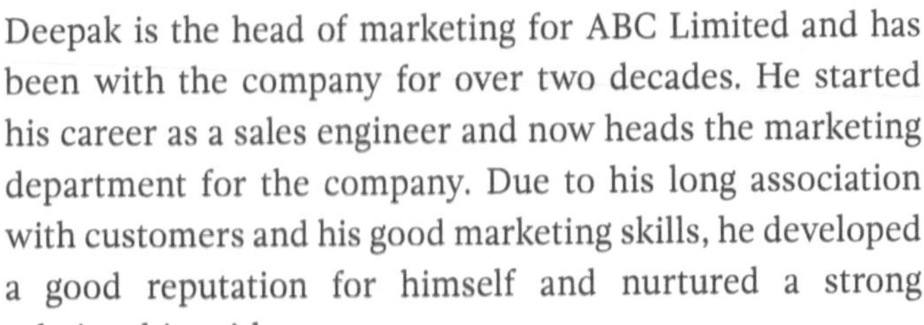

Deepak is the head of marketing for ABC Limited and has been with the company for over two decades. He started his career as a sales engineer and now heads the marketing department for the company. Due to his long association with customers and his good marketing skills, he developed a good reputation for himself and nurtured a strong relationship with customers.

ABC Limited operates in a B2B segment. It manufactures niche capital goods. There are only a few major clients. Vishal knows that it is very important that he has direct contact with key customers. Hence, he went along with Deepak and met the key customers. Such visits also provided a good opportunity to learn how well Deepak is connected with the customers.

After visiting major customers, Vishal understood ABC has a strong reputation with clients. In addition, the Sales Team headed by Deepak enjoyed a strong relationship with customers. Vishal congratulated Deepak on his bond with the customers.

Vishal started his favorite topic of how Deepak could improve his performance. Various topics like increasing the price of the product, removing the credit terms, expanding the geography, etc. were discussed. Deepak vehemently opposed any price increase to the product as it would impact the market share of the product. As a typical marketing person, he said that the Purchase team should be pushed hard to buy at lower costs. Vishal being a mature person told Deepak to stay focused on his functional area (marketing).

To impress upon Deepak, how his team could improve the financial performance of the company, Vishal illustrated with the help of the following P&L prepared by him as an example. He increased the revenue by 1% as a representation of a 1% increase in the selling price of the products.

Vishal explained to Deepak that a mere increase of 1% in the sales price can increase

• the PBT from Rs. 2041 Mn to Rs. 2306 Mn which is an increase of 13%.

• The earnings per share will go up from Rs. 43.99 to Rs. 49.70.

• The ROCE will go up from 37.66% to 42.23%

• The ROE will go up from 39.70% to 44.85%

No.	Description	Formula	Rs. Mn		Scenario 1
					Increase in Selling Price
A	Revenue from operations		26,500		26,765
B	Direct Material cost		19,978	75.4%	19,978
C	Employee Benefit		1,345		1,345
D	Manufacturing expense		1,836	6.9%	1,836
E	Sales & Admin expense		529	2.0%	529
F	Gross Margin	A-B-C-D-E	2,812		3,077
G	Depreciation		631		631
H	Margin after Depreciation	F-G	2,181		2,446
I	Interest payment		140		140
J	Profit before Tax	H-I	2,041		2,306
K	Tax		510		577
L	Profit after tax	J-K	1,531	5.8%	1,730
	Earnings per Share		43.99		49.70
	ROCE		37.66%		42.23%
	ROE		39.70%		44.85%

Though Deepak is convinced that a mere increase of 1% can contribute to a big impact on the financials of the company, he knows that it is not easy.

Having explained the impact, Vishal was confident that the above thought would work in the subconscious mind of Deepak and he would find ways to convince the customer on a price hike.

> I would like to mention here that a price increase of a product in the market is not determined only by the company that sells the product but also by the market forces; i.e the competition and the supply and demand situation. Sometimes the marketing team assumes that any price increase will result in loss of orders. This may not be true and hence it is sensible to examine this regularly. How do we do this? Study the market and the competitor offering in terms of price and benefits and compare with your product and make a judgement on whether your product deserves a better price. Informal chat with the customers can reveal whether the customer is willing to pay that extra money or not.

Having sowed the seed of price increase in Deepak's subconscious mind, he moves on to his next agenda, "the payment collection".

Being in a capital goods industry, ABC's typical payment terms are as follows

• 30% down payment along with the order

• 60% payment after 30 days of supply of the equipment, and

• final 10% after the commissioning of the equipment, which normally takes 90 days.

Vishal talks to Deepak about changing the payment terms to "pay and take" the machine. This means the customer pays the money upfront and then collects the machine. This saves a lot of work on the follow-up for the payment and improves the cash flow a lot. Obviously, Deepak was not in favour of this.

It is normal that customers will not be willing to change the payment terms that has been established and being practiced for several years. So, it is important to understand how the industry operates. I know of a company which was selling their product on credit and it used to be a huge task collecting the outstanding from multiple customers. The marketing department never agreed that they could change the payment terms. However, the corporate headquarters of the company decided that they will sell only after collecting the payment and was ready to face any reduction in sales. This was a calculated move after understanding the reputation of the product in the market. This made a huge change in the fortune of the company though there was a dip in the sale for a temporary period. Once this company standardized on "pay and take" mode of payment their competitors also moved over to this payment terms and the whole industry corrected it's terms of payment.

Vishal did not want to push Deepak on this. Hence he looked at the "Outstanding Collection" performance of Deepak's team.

While reviewing the outstanding, Vishal observed that on average there is a delay of 15 days in the payment collection from the customers. Vishal raised a strong objection to this. Since the agreed payment term with the customers was 30 days, it is only right for ABC Limited to expect the payment on the 30th day. Why should this be received after 45 days? Deepak had no answer for this. It was a regular practice that his team followed up with the customer after the completion of 30 days and it took a couple of weeks or more before the payment was realized from the customers.

Vishal illustrated the following.

The annual sales revenue for the company was Rs. 26,500 Mn. This amount is collected from the customer in the form of advance payment, supply payment, and the final retention payment. From the records it is found that there is a delay of 15 days, on average on all these payments from the due date.

If this payment of Rs 26,500 Mn had been collected exactly on the due date, the cash could have flowed into the company much earlier and the company could have reduced the borrowings from the bank and thus saved the interest payment.

The interest being paid by the company for the working capital was at 10% per annum. If the Rs 26,500 million is received 15 days earlier, the interest saved would be

(Amount X Interest pa) X (no. of days/ 365 days)
(26500 X10%)*(15/365) = Rs. 108.90 Mn

It is not practical to collect the payment exactly on the due date, as customers may have a practice of paying on a certain specific day of the week (as the payment day), or there could be some other lapses. Hence Vishal agreed with Deepak that the marketing team would ensure that the average delay to collect payment would be within seven days. Hence there is a saving of 8 days (15 days -7 days) of interest due to the increased cash flow.

(26500 X10%)*(8/365) = Rs. 58.1 Mn
Giving the effect of the above to the P&L, let us see what happens

No.	Description	Formula	Rs. Mn		Scenario 2 reduction of delay in Collection of
A	Revenue from operations		26,500		26,500
B	Direct Material cost		19,978	75.4%	19,978
C	Employee Benefit		1,345		1,345
D	Manufacturing expense		1,836	6.9%	1,836
E	Sales & Admin expense		529	2.0%	529
F	Gross Margin	A-B-C-D-E	2,812		2,812
G	Depreciation		631		631
H	Margin after Depreciation	F-G	2,181		2,181
I	Interest payment		140		82
J	Profit before Tax	H-I	2,041		2,099
K	Tax		510		525
L	Profit after tax	J-K	1,531	5.9%	1,574
	Earnings per Share		43.99		45.24
	ROCE		37.66%		37.66%
	ROE		39.70%		40.83%

The interest payment reduced from Rs 140 Mn to Rs 82 Mn resulting in an increase of profit before tax from Rs. 2041 Mn to Rs. 2099 Mn. The profit after tax moved up from Rs 1531 Mn to Rs 1574 Mn.

The above changes increased the earnings per share by more than Rs. 1 and the return on equity by about 1.1 percentage points.

Vishal promised Deepak that he would not insist on any initiative that would damage the reputation of the company or the product. He also assured Deepak that he would work alongside Deepak in this endevour since he understood that even a small slip would spoil the business.

The frequent discussions between Vishal and Deepak helped forge a strong relationship between them based on mutual respect. This helped them to discuss freely to improve the performance of the company further.

They decided to deep dive into the sales segmentation i.e. sales by product segment.

ABC Limited sells 4 types of products. Let's say Product A, Product B, Product C, and Product D. With the help of the finance team Vishal and Deepak conducted a Cost audit and identified the direct variable cost that goes into making these products. It consisted of direct material cost and the direct manufacturing cost.

The difference between the selling price and the direct variable cost (the direct material cost plus direct manufacturing cost) may be called the "Contribution Margin".

It's normal that each of these products has a different contribution %. From this contribution amount, the company pays for the fixed expenses of the company, the interest, and the depreciation and other costs. What remains after that is the profit.

On examining the various products that the company makes, the finance team published the following table.

Sales segmentation	Sales Rs. Mn (A)	DMC (B)	Direct MFG Cost (C)	Total cost (D= B+C)	Contribution (E=A-D)	Contribution % (E/A *100)
Product A	12000	9240	840	10080	1920	16.0%
Product B	6000	4860	360	5220	780	13.0%
Product C	5000	3600	250	3850	1150	23.0%
Product D	3500	2278	175	2453	1047	29.9%
	26500	19978	1625	21603	4897	18.5%

Product A which contributed to 45% of the sales had a contribution margin of 16%.

Product D which contributed to 13% of the sales had the highest contribution margin of Rs. 29.9%.

Product B had the lowest contribution of 13%.

Hypothetically speaking the company could stop manufacturing product B and utilize this capacity towards increasing the sale of product D. But this may not be practical as there could be other limitations in the market, for example;

- the total demand for product D may be very low and the company ABC may enjoy more than 50% market share and it is highly impossible to increase the market share beyond it. Or,
- the market size of product D is very big and actually the company ABC is enjoying just about 2 to 3% market share because it is charging a much higher price compared to its competitors and hence increasing the sale of product D may be very difficult.

Based on the above table Vishal urged Deepak to review the market condition and devise a plan to increase the sale of product D or product C so that the margin for the company increases. Since ABC has a limitation in terms of its production capacity, Vishal told Deepak that a reduction in the sale of Product B or Product A can be considered if the sale of Product D could be increased.

Due to his good understanding of the market and the product, Deepak was reasonably convinced that he could increase the sales of product D by 10%, i.e. from Rs 3500 Mn to Rs 3850 Mn. Since the factory has a limited production capacity, the increase in the volume of product D should have a matched reduction in the production of some other products. Deepak proposed to reduce the sale of product B to the extent of Rs 300 Mn.

Based on the above thoughts of Deepak, Vishal prepared the revised segmented sale for ABC Limited and was happy to see that the contribution increased by Rs 65.7 Mn, i.e. from Rs 4897 Mn to Rs. 4963 Mn. The same is explained in the table below.

Scenario 3

Sales segmentation	Sales Rs. Mn (A)	DMC (B)	Direct MFG Cost (C)	Total cost (D= B+C)	Contribution % from the above table (E)	Contribution Rs. Mn (A * E)	Increase/ Decrease in Sale
Product A	12000.0	9240.0	840.0	10080.0	16.0%	1920.0	
Product B	5700.0	4617.0	342.0	4959.0	13.0%	741.0	-5%
Product C	5000.0	3600.0	250.0	3850.0	23.0%	1150.0	
Product D	3850.0	2505.8	192.5	2698.3	29.9%	1151.7	10%
	26550.0	19962.8	1624.5	21587.3		4962.7	
Increase in Contribution						65.7	

Now let us see the impact of the above revised segmented sales on the P&L Statement.

No.	Description	Formula	Rs. Mn		Scenario 3 change in sales portfolio
A	Income from operations		26,500		26,550
B	Direct Material cost		19,978	75.4%	19,963
C	Employee Benefit		1,345		1,345
D	Manufacturing expense		1,836	6.9%	1,836
E	Sales & Admin expense		529	2.0%	529
F	Gross Margin	A-B-C-D-E	2,812		2,877
G	Depreciation		631		631
H	Margin after Depreciation	F-G	2,181		2,246
I	Interest payment		140		140
J	Profit before Tax	H-I	2,041		2,106
K	Tax		510		527
L	Profit after tax	J-K	1,531	5.8%	1,580
	Earnings per Share		43.99		45.39
	ROCE		37.66%		38.78%
	ROE		39.70%		40.97%

You may observe that the profit before tax increased from Rs. 2041 Mn to Rs. 2106 Mn, which is Rs. 65 Mn. We have seen that the contribution has increased by Rs. 65.7 Mn. The difference of Rs. 0.7 Mn is on account of rounding off to the higher digits hence kindly ignore this difference. The impact is as follows.

The PAT increased from Rs 1531 Mn to Rs. 1580 Mn.
The EPS increased from Rs 43.99 to Rs 45.39.
The ROCE increased from 37.66% to 38.78%
The ROE increased from 39.7 % to 40.97%

This is a significant improvement in the financials of the company.

Vishal consolidated the various possibilities that were discussed with Deepak, viz;

• Increase in selling price by 1%
• Reduction in the delay of collection from an average of 15 days to an average of 7 days
• Increasing the sale of product D by reducing the sale of product B

The result was astounding.
The PAT increased by Rs. 291 Mn (from Rs 1531 Mn to Rs 1822 Mn). an increase of 19 %
In terms of PAT % on Sales, it increased from 5.8% to 6.8%,
The earnings per share increased from Rs. 43.99 to Rs 52.37.
The ROCE increased from 37.66% to 43.36%
The ROE increased from 39.7% to 47.26%

No.	Description	Formula	Rs. Mn		Scenario 1 Increase in Selling Price	Scenario 2 reduction of delay in Collection of payments	Scenario 3 change in sales portfolio		All 3 scenarios	
A	Revenue from operations		26,500		26,765	26,500	26,550		26,816	
B	Direct Material cost		19,978		19,978	19,978	19,963		19,963	
C	Employee Benefit		1,345		1,345	1,345	1,345		1,345	
D	Manufacturing expense		1,836		1,836	1,836	1,836		1,836	
E	Sales & Admin expense		529		529	529	529		529	
F	Gross Margin	A-B-C-D-E	2,812		3,077	2,812	2,877		3,143	
G	Depreciation		631		631	631	631		631	
H	Margin after Depreciation	F-G	2,181		2,446	2,181	2,246		2,512	
I	Interest payment		140		140	82	140		82	
J	Profit before Tax	H-I	2,041		2,306	2,099	2,106		2,430	
K	Tax		510		577	525	527		607	
L	Profit after tax	J-K	1,531	5.8%	1,730	1,574	1,580		1,822	6.8%
	Earnings per Share		43.99		49.70	45.24	45.39		52.37	
	ROCE		37.66%		42.23%	37.66%	38.78%		43.36%	
	ROE		39.70%		44.85%	40.83%	40.97%		47.26%	

Deepak was awe-struck at the huge impact that he & his team could make on the financials of the company. He jumped into the action immediately.

Vishal was happy that he could motivate his marketing team and convince them of the big potential in front of them. He was sure that the team would go all out to meet this projected improvement in the financials.

Snippet - 7

The **Great Depression (1929–1939)** *is widely regarded as the worst financial crisis in world history due to its massive economic, social, and political impact globally. Here's an overview of why it holds this distinction:*

- *Global GDP shrank by approximately **15%** (by comparison, the 2008 Financial Crisis saw a 1% decline globally).*
- *Unemployment soared, reaching **25%** in the U.S. and similarly high levels in other industrialized nations.*
- *Thousands of banks failed (9,000 in the U.S. alone), wiping out savings for millions of people.*
- *Credit dried up, stalling investment and consumer spending.*
- *The crisis began with the U.S. stock market crash on October 29, 1929 (known as "Black Tuesday").*
- *This triggered a panic among investors, leading to a rapid decline in wealth.*
- *Prices fell sharply, reducing business revenues and wages while increasing the burden of debt, further deepening the crisis.*
- *Farmers, already struggling, were particularly hard-hit as crop prices plummeted.*
- *The crisis quickly spread beyond the U.S., affecting Europe, Latin America, and Asia.*

Brain GYM – III

1. Deepak attempted to increase the sale of Product D by 10% by sacrificing the sale of Product B. However, in reality, the sales of Product B fell by 6% and the sales of Product D increased by 5% only. What will be the impact on P&L. Assume that there was no change in the manufacturing cost.

2. In an attempt to increase the sales price of the products, the marketing team ended up with the following situation, while retaining the quantity of sale as the same. Prepare the P&L.

- Price of Product A increased by 0.5%
- Price of Product B increased by 1%
- Price of Product C decreased by 0.5%
- There is no change in the price of Product D

CHAPTER SEVEN

PRODUCTION

"Where ideas take shape—turning visions into tangible realities with precision and care."

Anil Sharma heads the manufacturing team at ABC Limited. He is a typical shop floor man with many years of experience in fabrication, machining, and assembly areas. After his diploma in engineering, he started his career as a machine operator. He grew over the years to head the company's production department.

He had excellent command over his team, earning their respect through his deep knowledge and exceptional interpersonal skills. He thrives on taking on complex projects and executing them with precision and confidence.

He generally does not mingle with his peers from other departments. He's always engrossed in his area of work.

When Vishal visited the shop floor for the first time, he was quite impressed with Anil's work. To build a rapport with Anil, Vishal scheduled weekly visits to the shop floor to understand his potential.

After a while, Vishal asked Anil about his opinion on his contribution to the company. Anil said, "Vishal Ji I have nothing special to contribute. I execute whatever job is scheduled in our shop to the best of my ability. Beyond this, I don't have any special role."

Vishal replied, "Anil I'm quite impressed with the knowledge and skill you possess and the passion with which you do your job. I am also impressed by the respect you command from your team."

Vishal continued, "You might have heard from your other colleagues that I am focusing on improving the financials of the company by working with individual departments. In continuation of that, I would like to work with you to leverage the potential in your area for improving the financial performance of the company."

Anil was not used to thinking beyond manufacturing. For the first time, he felt like he was part of the management and was enthused to work with Vishal. He said, "Vishal ji, no one has treated me as an important link in the chain of the company. I was always told to do the job as scheduled by the Planning Department. I never thought about the possibility of doing something better that could shore up the performance of the company. I am more than happy to do something that would improve the financials of the company, but you need to help me."

Vishal was happy to hear this and said, "Let's kickstart our activities."

Anil, you're an expert in your area and I cannot advise you on the initiatives for your function. However, I could ask you certain questions based on which you could review your functional area.

Vishal continued, "There are several machines (resources) in our production floor. Identify the critical machine that decides the output of your shop. In such a machine, check whether you can improve the efficiency of the machine, by reducing the time it takes to process a component."

Vishal gifted a "Theory of Constraint" a book by Eliyahu Goldratt to Anil and asked him to go through the book. With all sincerity, Anil read the book and understood the concepts provided.

The first job that Anil took up was to identify the bottleneck in his operations which if removed can push up the productivity.

He had a doubt, what is the point in pushing the productivity when marketing department is not demanding a higher production? With this question, he met Vishal to clarify the same since Vishal had promised that he could walk into his room at any time and get clarifications on the mission that they are working together. Vishal explained to Anil that there are several benefits of creating capacity.

1. The marketing department can be pushed for a higher order booking.
2. The subcontracting of certain components can be stopped and the same can be manufactured in-house.
3. If there is a substantial increase in productivity, the number of shifts can be reduced. In addition, the idle assets may be sold thus reducing the asset in the Balance Sheet and creating space in the shop floor.

Vishal said, "Let us not go into selling assets and reducing manpower. Let us stay focused on reducing the cycle time and thus provide an opportunity for the marketing department to book more orders and/or reduce sub-contracting costs by bringing some parts back for in-house machining."

With the help of the planning department, Anil identified the first constraint i.e. the first work center that was deciding the total output of the company. He studied the operations being performed in that machine and looked at the following options.

1. Improving the speed and feed of cutting tools thus reducing the manufacturing time of several components made on the shop floor. This is possible by using many modern tools.
2. Possibility of shifting some of the components that are manufactured in this machine tool to some other machine that is not fully loaded
3. Reducing the loading and unloading time through better clamping.

Once Anil de-bottlenecked one machine, the constraint moved to another machine. Anil started working on that work center as well. This continued till Anil was satisfied that he had reasonably exhausted all the possibilities. Now, he discussed with the Planning and Purchase department to understand what are the manufactured parts that are being subcontracted or outsourced. From that list of components, he chose those items that were more suitable for his machines and started manufacturing them.

The potential cost savings by bringing these parts from sub-contracting to in-house machining worked out to Rs. 200 Mn. Thus, the cost of subcontracting for a financial year could be reduced by Rs. 200 Mn. This results in the reduction of material cost from Rs. 19978 Mn to Rs. 19778 Mn.

Anil had to spend Rs. 50 Mn towards new consumables that he would need for machining these new parts. This would increase the cost of manufacturing from Rs. 1836 Mn to Rs. 1886 Mn.

With this information, he discussed with the finance team and requested them to prepare financials incorporating this improvement. The finance team gave him the following comparison.

Description	Formula	Rs. Mn		Scenario 1 reduction in Sub-contract
Revenue from operations		26,500		26,500
Direct Material cost		19,978		19,778
Employee Benefit		1,345		1,345
Manufacturing expense		1,836		1,886
Sales & Admin expense		529		529
Gross Margin	A-B-C-D-E	2,812		2,962
Depreciation		631		631
Margin after Depreciation	F-G	2,181		2,331
Interest payment		140		140
Profit before Tax (PBT)	H-I	2,041	7.7%	2,191
Tax		510		548
Profit after tax (PAT)	J-K	1,531		1,643
Earnings per Share		43.99		47.22
ROCE		37.66%		40.25%
ROE		39.70%		42.62%

With this good news, Anil rushed to meet Vishal. Vishal was busy with Syed the Plant Engineering manager trying to convince him of the potential he has in improving the performance of the company.

Anil impatiently waited to meet Vishal. After Syed left, he rushed inside and showed him the above table. He thanked Vishal for igniting his interest in an area that he never looked at before. He proudly presented that he could increase the profit before tax from Rs 2041 Mn to Rs 2191 Mn i.e. from 7.7% to 8.3%.

The Earnings per share increased from Rs. 43.99 to Rs 47.22.

The ROCE increased from 37.66% to 40.25%

The ROE increased from 39.70% to 42.62%

Vishal was very happy to see the enthusiasm of Anil and the potential improvement in the financials of the company. He congratulated Anil. Anil asked, "Is there anything else that I could do?". Vishal pointed out, "You could see from the table the manufacturing expense is Rs 1886 Mn. If you manage to save 1%, it will be Rs 19 Mn. This would directly boost the profit before tax to Rs 2210 Mn instead of Rs 2191 Mn. This would increase the percentage of profit from 8.3% to 8.37%. Anil promised to work on this line as well.

Anil was curious to know about the reduction in assets that was mentioned by Vishal in his previous discussions and requested Vishal to explain the same.

Vishal created the following table to explain to Anil.

	Balance Sheet			reduced Asset
No	**Description**	**Rs. Mn**	**Rs. Mn**	**Rs. Mn**
a	Equity Share capital		348.0	348.0
b	Reserves and Surplus		3,508.0	3,508.0
A	Total shareholders funds	a+b	3,856.0	3,856.0
c	Long term borrowings		1,211.0	911.0
d	Other liabilities and long term provisions		725.0	725.0
B	Total non current liabilities	c+d	1,936.0	1,636.0
e	Short term borrowings		1,033.0	1,033.0
f	Trade payables		4,130.0	4,130.0
g	Other current liabilities and provision		845.0	845.0
C	Total current liabilities	e+f+g	6,008.0	6,008.0
	Grand total of liabilities	**A+B+C**	**11,800.0**	**11,500.0**
	Assets			
h	Tangible assets		6,260.0	5,960.0
i	Intangible asset		688.0	688.0
j	Capital WIP		574.0	574.0
k	Other financial assets		611.0	611.0
D	Total non current asset	h+i+j+k	8,133.0	7,833.0
m	Current investments		191.0	191.0
n	Inventories		1,236.0	1,236.0
o	Trade receivables		955.0	955.0
p	Cash and cash equivalents		242.0	242.0
q	Other current assets		1,043.0	1,043.0
E	Total current assets	m+n+o+p+q	3,667.0	3,667.0
	Grand total of the asset	D+E	11,800.0	11,500.0

Vishal started from the balance sheet. He explained, let's assume that you can release a few assets that are valued at Rs 300 Mn, as per the company records. When this gets sold, the tangible assets will reduce from Rs. 6260 Mn to Rs 5960 Mn. When this money flows into the company, the Long-Term Borrowings could be repaid to the same extent thus reducing it from Rs 1211 Mn to Rs 911 Mn.

Anil intervened, "Vishal ji, how does it help to improve the profitability? Vishal said, "Now let's go to the Profit

& Loss statement. Since the long-term borrowings are reduced, the interest payment will be reduced. Assuming 10% as the interest, it will bring down the total interest paid from Rs 140 Mn to Rs 110 Mn. In addition, the depreciation will reduce from Rs. 631 Mn to Rs. 601 Mn. The net effect of all this will increase the profit before tax from Rs 2041 Mn to Rs. 2101Mn.

Description	Formula	Rs. Mn		Scenario 2 reduced asset
Revenue from operations		26,500		26,500
Direct Material cost		19,978		19,978
Employee Benefit		1,345		1,345
Manufacturing expense		1,836		1,836
Sales & Admin expense		529		529
Gross Margin	A-B-C-D-E	2,812		2,812
Depreciation		631		601
Margin after Depreciation	F-G	2,181		2,211
Interest payment		140		110
Profit before Tax (PBT)	H-I	2,041	7.7%	2,101
Tax		510		525
Profit after tax (PAT)	J-K	1,531		1,576
Earnings per Share		43.99		45.28
ROCE		37.66%		40.26%
ROE		39.70%		40.86%

In addition,

The earnings per share will increase from Rs. 43.99 to Rs 45.28.

The ROCE will increase from 37.66% to 40.26%

The ROE will increase from 39.70% to 40.86%.

Vishal continued, "In addition to the above, the income from the sale of the asset will figure as an extraordinary income in the Profit & Loss statement and shore up the profit for the particular year. However, let us not bother about that as it is a one-time income."

Anil was very happy to learn the above and thanked Vishal for teaching him. He was determined to work in this direction.

Snippet - 8

Large, established companies known for their strong financial stability and consistent performance are referred to as Blue Chip companies in the stock market. These companies are considered the "safest bets" in the investment world. Examples include companies like Apple, Coca-Cola, Larsen & Toubro and Reliance Industries.

*The term **"blue chip"** originates from the game of poker, where chips of different colors are used to represent varying monetary values. Traditionally, blue chips held the highest value in the game.*

The term was first used in the 1920s by Oliver Gingold, an employee of Dow Jones.

He observed that stocks trading at $200 or more per share were often from elite, high-value companies and referred to them as "blue-chip stocks."

Brain GYM – IV

1. Prepare a P&L if Rs. 350 Mn of sub-contracting could be moved to in-house machining. For performing this additional work, the company spends Rs. 75 Mn extra on Manufacturing expenses and Rs. 5 Mn extra on employee costs.

2. ABC Limited decides to pay an extra-ordinary dividend of Rs. 5 per share utilising the cash available at the end of the year. The amount will be Rs. 5 * 34.8 Mn shares. Prepare the balance sheet and also calculate the EPS, ROCE, and ROE with the changed balance sheet but with the original P&L which shows a PAT of Rs. 1531 Mn.

CHAPTER EIGHT

FINANCE

"The heartbeat of the business—measuring, guiding, and fueling every decision toward sustainable success."

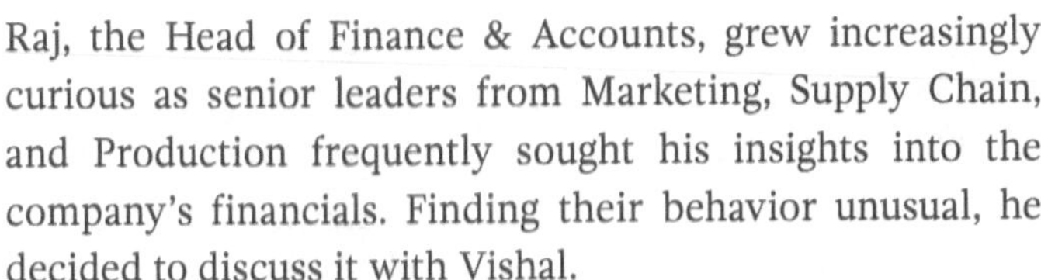

Raj, the Head of Finance & Accounts, grew increasingly curious as senior leaders from Marketing, Supply Chain, and Production frequently sought his insights into the company's financials. Finding their behavior unusual, he decided to discuss it with Vishal.

"Sir, I would like to tell you that in recent months Senior people from Marketing, Supply Chain, and Production have been contacting me to understand the financial terms and asking me to create P&L, BS, and CF scenarios based on some assumptions by them. I would like to bring this to your notice as this is something that has not been happening in the past. The department leaders never used to bother about the bottom line, return on capital employed, or return on equity."

Vishal explained what he has been doing with every function and added, "I strongly believe that the financials of a company are built by every individual and not just by the CEO".

Raj asked, "Sir do I also have a role in improving the financial parameters of the company? I was restricting my role to maintaining strict adherence to the statutory requirement and following good accounting practices."

"Raj, I thought I would come to you at the end, after discussing with all the other departments about their possible role in improving the financial parameters of the company. Now that you have come on your own, let's have a short discussion. As you are a finance person, I think it will be much easier", said Vishal.

"Raj can you share your cash flow projection for this year", asked Vishal. Refer to the cashflow statement on the next page.

After looking at the statement, Vishal asked, "Why do we have a large closing balance for several months during the year? Is it possible that we repay our short-term loans? This would save some interest cost".

"Sir, I do not suggest this since these cash balances are highly fluctuating and as you can see in some of the months, they are less than Rs 10 Mn. If we use this money to repay short-term loans, then we will lose the flexibility in our payments to our creditors. As you may know Sir, we are enjoying a good reputation on timely payments to our vendors", said Raj.

"You're right and I agree with you that we should have certain flexibility in our payments. However, may I suggest that we park our funds in Mutual Funds that can be taken out as and when required by us? At the same time, these funds earn certain dividends/ interest", replied Vishal.

"Sir, as per the policy of the company we are not supposed to invest our funds in any speculative investments and hence I did not consider that as an option" replied Raj.

Cash Flow												
Inflow Rs. Mn	Apr	May	Jun	Jul	Aug	Sep	Oct	Nov	Dec	Jan	Feb	Mar
Opening balance	242	464	687	682	706	849	4	8	133	3	8	103
Customer collection	2208	2208	2208	2208	2208	2208	2208	2208	2208	2208	2208	2208
working capital loan												
Outflow												
Vendor payment	1665	1665	1665	1665	1665	1665	1665	1665	1665	1665	1665	1665
salary and wages	112	112	112	112	112	112	112	112	112	112	112	112
Manufacturing expenses	153	153	153	153	153	153	153	153	153	153	153	153
Sales & Admin expenses	44	44	44	44	44	44	44	44	44	44	44	44
interest payment LT loan	6	6	6	6	6	6	6	6	6	6	6	6
interest payment WC loan	6	6	6	5	5	5	4	4	4	3	3	3
loan repayment			150			150			150			150
Statutory payment - Tax			77			154			154			128
Dividends						765						
capital investment				200	80		220	100	50	220	130	
Closing balance	464	687	682	706	849	4	8	133	3	8	103	50

Vishal explained, "I agree with you that we are not in the business of speculation but at the same time we can invest in non-negative funds like debt funds where the returns are less but there is no possibility of reduction of principal. We can even invest for a few days in such mutual funds. Whenever the money is not required for the next 7 days, they can be invested for just a week".

Vishal continued, "Let us look at a hypothetical scenario. Let us consider that the Cash balance at the end of the month is available throughout the month. Let us retain Rs 50 Mn as emergency cash and for anything over and above Rs 50 Mn let's invest in non-negative funds. For example, in April Rs 464 Mn is shown as the cash balance. Leaving out Rs. 50 Mn for emergency we can invest Rs 414 Mn in funds that could generate about 6% interest. If Rs. 414 Mn was invested for 30 days we could earn Rs 2.07 Mn as interest. Likewise, if you do this for every month the total income that the finance department could generate will be Rs 16.37 Mn.

Alternatively,

If you take the average cash balance for the 12 months, it comes to Rs. 308 Mn. (Sum of cash balance/ 12). If we remove Rs. 200 Mn from April and use it to repay the long-term borrowings, the interest burden will come down thus reducing the interest payout by Rs. 20 Mn (10% of Rs. 200 Mn). The average cash balance will be Rs. 108 Mn (Rs. 308 Mn – Rs. 200 Mn). However, some of the months will have a negative cash balance since we removed Rs. 200 Mn in April. But let's assume that we can manage the negative months by postponing certain expenses.

Cash Flow

Inflow Rs. Mn	Apr	May	Jun	Jul	Aug	Sep	Oct	Nov	Dec	Jan	Feb	Mar
Opening balance	242	464	687	682	706	849	4	8	133	3	8	103
Customer collection	2208	2208	2208	2208	2208	2208	2208	2208	2208	2208	2208	2208
working capital loan	0	0	0	0	0	0	0	0	0	0	0	0
Outflow												
Vendor payment	1665	1665	1665	1665	1665	1665	1665	1665	1665	1665	1665	1665
salary and wages	112	112	112	112	112	112	112	112	112	112	112	112
Manufacturing expenses	153	153	153	153	153	153	153	153	153	153	153	153
Sales & Admin expenses	44	44	44	44	44	44	44	44	44	44	44	44
interest payment LT loan	6	6	6	6	6	6	6	6	6	6	6	6
interest payment WC loan	6	6	6	5	5	5	4	4	4	3	3	3
loan repayment	0	0	150	0	0	150	0	0	150	0	0	150
Statutory payment - Tax	0	0	77	0	0	154	0	0	154	0	0	128
Dividends	0	0	0	0	0	765	0	0	0	0	0	0
capital investment	0	0	0	200	80	0	220	100	50	220	130	
Closing balance	464	687	682	706	849	4	8	133	3	8	103	50
Interest that could be earned by parking the excess fund in Bank @ 6%	2.07	3.18	3.16	3.28	4.00			0.41			0.27	
Total												16.37

This sounded interesting to Raj and he felt inclusive in improving the financial performance of the company.

Raj had an idea regarding the use of excess funds and asked Vishal about it.

"Sir, I would like to ask your opinion on this idea. We have been buying materials on 60 days credit. Whenever we have excess cash in a month why don't we pay these vendors in advance by deducting interest for early payment at the rate of say 8%? Most of our vendors may not have access to funds at 8%. This not only helps us to get returns with our excess cash but also helps the vendor in their cash management".

Vishal was very happy to hear this from Raj. He said, "Yes, that's quite possible. I suggest you talk to the supply chain team and identify vendors who may need such support. In fact, this is better than investing in Mutual Funds since the interest earned will be more than 6% and also provides support to our vendors in their cash management.

Raj asked, "Sir, is there anything else that I could do?".

Vishal highlighted the following point.

"One thing that I've seen in the financials of the previous years is that there are certain unpredictable impacts of foreign exchange variations in our financials when compared to the assumptions made at the time of budget exercise. Since we have significant exports in our Sales, we are exposed to the foreign exchange variations. In certain years we end up with higher profits because of the weakening of our currency and in certain other years, we end up with lower profits due to the weakening of the currency in which we are making our sales. This is because we are not taking forward cover for our exports and imports.

I (the author of the book) get reminded of what our Corporate CFO told us during one of the worst financial crises, 20 years ago. "Guys, I find that some of our Business Units are not taking due care when they do business in foreign currencies. The business units are not taking forward cover for the foreign exchange exposure. They expect Rupee to weaken by the time they get payment from the customers. Thus, the units expects to make additional income compared to what was anticipated at the time of order booking or at the time of budgeting.

But this need not be true always. Sometimes Rupee strengthens. During such a scenario, the units will lose money. I urge our businesses not to indulge in speculation of the currencies. Whenever you finalise a contract with a foreign customer, you do it based on prevailing exchange rate and an acceptable margin at that exchange rate. You should immediately take forward cover for that exposure both in terms of exports and imports. This ensures that you make the planned the margin. Even if the currency weakens or strengthens it will not have any impact on the projected profitability of your business.

Vishal was also of a similar opinion as explained in the above insert and hence he gave the same Gyan to Raj. He ended by saying, "This practice will ensure that there's no uncertainties in the financials. You may lose certain potential earnings when some currencies weaken but never get lured by this and start speculating".

Goods & Service Tax (GST) was brought in by the Government to avoid Tax on Tax. When a company buys a material from a Supplier it pays to the Vendor, the value of the material and also GST on it.

Using this material, the company makes a product by adding value. When the company sells the product to its customer, it claims from the customer GST on the value added product. However, it pays to the government only the amount that is in excess of the GST that it paid to the material it purchased from its vendor

For eg.

The company purchased material for Rs. 100. It paid 18% as GST i.e Rs.18.

(The GST that the company paid for the input material will remain as credit in the name of the company (with the Government) until it is used for paying the value added product that it sells to its customers in India.)

Using this material, it manufactured a product and sold it for Rs. 300. This product will also attract a GST of say 18%. i.e. Rs. 54. The company will collect Rs. 354 from the customer.

However, while remitting the GST it collected from the customer (i.e. Rs. 54), the company will deduct Rs. 18 which it already paid while buying the material. It will remit only Rs. 36 (54-18).

When the company has substantial export sales this Tax credit can not be used, since there is no Tax applicable for export sales.

In such a case, this amount accumulates at the government coffers. Realising this cash burden on the businesses, the government allows the companies to pay tax on export and claim the same as refund by providing certain documents, i.e the government allows this money to be withdrawn and used for business by following certain procedures.

Raj reminded Vishal, "Sir you said there are a couple of points, what is your next point". Yeah, I will come to that said Vishal. "In the Balance Sheet, I see that we have Rs. 1043 Mn in other current assets. Can you let me know the breakup of the same?" Raj replied that a significant portion of this (over Rs. 500 Mn) is with the government as the Tax Credit which will be utilised for paying GST to Government when the company makes Domestic sales. Since the company had a good amount of exports in the previous years the credit has accumulated.

Vishal asked Raj to investigate this and ensure that only the amount required to meet the next 1 month's Tax requirement is kept with the Government. In the current scenario, out of Rs 1043 Mn current assets Rs. 500 Mn is on account of tax credit. Let's assume that Rs 200 Mn can be taken out as a GST refund and can be used to pay back the short-term loans, which are at the rate of 10% interest. Over one year, it can easily save an interest payment of Rs 20 Mn.

With this input, Vishal told Raj, "I hope I shared a few tips on possible contributions to the bottom line of the company. The money earned by investing in funds could result in earnings of Rs 16.37 Mn and reducing the tax credit could potentially save an interest payment of Rs. 20 Mn. Together it makes about Rs. 36 Mn for the year." You can see the impact of the same in the following table.

No.	Description	Formula	Rs. Mn	Scenario 1 invest excess fund	Scenario 2 repaying borrowing
	Revenue from operations		26,500	26,500	26,500
	Other income			16	
A	Total Income		26,500	26,516	26,500
B	Direct Material cost		19,978	19,978	19,978
C	Employee Benefit		1,345	1,345	1,345
D	Manufacturing expense		1,836	1,836	1,836
E	Sales & Admin expense		529	529	529
F	Gross Margin	A-B-C-D-E	2,812	2,828	2,812
G	Depreciation		631	631	631
H	Margin after Depreciation	F-G	2,181	2,197	2,181
I	Interest payment		140	140	120
J	Profit before tax	H-I	2,041	2,057	2,061
K	Tax		510	514	515
L	Profit after tax	J-K	1,531	1,543	1,546
	Earnings per Share		31.89	32.15	32.20
	ROCE		37.66%	37.94%	39.00%
	ROE		39.70%	40.02%	40.09%

Raj was happy with the meeting and headed to his office feeling more inclusive rather than just an accounting person.

Snippet – 9

Triple-Bottom-Line (TBL) Accounting *is an approach to measuring a company's performance that goes beyond traditional financial metrics. It evaluates performance in* **three key dimensions:** **Profit (economic), People (social), and Planet (environmental)***. The concept emphasizes sustainable business practices by considering a company's impact on society and the environment alongside economic success.*

CHAPTER NINE

PLANT ENGINEERING

**"The unsung hero ensuring that innovation never stops
and production runs without a hitch."**

Syed is a friendly person who mingles with everyone in the organization. He is willing to learn new things and implement them. Due to his frequent interactions with his colleagues, he learned Vishal's focus area and decided that he should do something before Vishal called him for a discussion.

As the head of plant engineering, he is entrusted with the upkeep of all Machines and Utilities in the company. He understands that his contribution could be a reduction in maintenance expenses and increased availability of machines for the production department. He knows that by increasing the availability of machines to the production department, they could bring some of the outsourced components to in-house manufacturing.

He discussed the uptime of various machines with his team. He understands that almost all the critical machines are at their peak performance and any improvement on this will be difficult. He also understands that a small increase in the downtime of these machines could result in pushing some components from in-house to outsourcing and thus increasing the cost of subcontracting.

He along with his team decides to implement modern maintenance techniques for these machines. He collects data related to Condition Based Maintenance, application of IIoT (Industrial Internet of Things) to predict failures, monitoring the energy consumption of each motor (to deduct abnormalities in advance), etc. By incorporating sensors at various points on the critical machines and building a clear dashboard Syed understands that he can maintain the critical machines better. This would require a capital expenditure of Rs 75 Mn. He decided to propose this to Vishal when he called him for a meeting.

The expenditure of Rs. 75 Mn has 2 parts. Firstly in the tangible assets like sensors for Rs. 50 Mn and secondly in software including development of Dashboard at Rs. 25 Mn, which is an intangible asset. Accordingly, both will be reflected in the Balance Sheet.

He meets Raj and explains his thought and requests him to explain the impact of the above proposal. Now that Raj understands Vishal well, he prepared the impact on the P&L and BS, as below.

	Balance Sheet			investment in predictive maintenance
No	Description		Rs. Mn	Rs. Mn
a	Equity Share capital		348.0	348.0
b	Reserves and Surplus		3,508.0	3,508.0
A	Total shareholders funds	a+b	3,856.0	3,856.0
c	Long term borrowings		1,211.0	1,286.0
d	Other liabilities and long term provisions		725.0	725.0
B	Total non current liabilities	c+d	1,936.0	2,011.0
e	Short term borrowings		1,033.0	1,033.0
f	Trade payables		4,130.0	4,130.0
g	Other current liabilities and provision		845.0	845.0
C	Total current liabilities	e+f+g	6,008.0	6,008.0
	Grand total of liabilities	A+B+C	**11,800.0**	**11,875.0**
	Assets			
h	Tangible assets		6,260.0	6,310.0
i	Intangible asset		688.0	713.0
j	Capital WIP		574.0	574.0
k	Other financial assets		611.0	611.0
D	Total non current asset	h+i+j+k	8,133.0	8,208.0
m	Current investments		191.0	191.0
n	Inventories		1,236.0	1,236.0
o	Trade receivables		955.0	955.0
p	Cash and cash equivalents		242.0	242.0
q	Other current assets		1,043.0	1,043.0
E	Total current assets	m+n+o+p+q	3,667.0	3,667.0
	Grand total of the asset	D+E	11,800.0	11,875.0

You may observe that the Tangible asset has increased by Rs. 50 Mn from Rs. 6260 Mn to Rs. 6310 Mn. The Intangible asset has increased from Rs. 688 Mn to Rs. 713 Mn. This investment of Rs. 75 Mn is funded through borrowings. This will have an impact on the P&L in the form of interest and depreciation.

Assuming that the tangible assets are depreciated over 10 years and the intangible assets are depreciated over 5 years, the depreciation for this additional asset will be = 50/10+25/5 = Rs 10 Mn. Hence the depreciation will go up from Rs. 631 Mn to Rs. 641 Mn.

Since the acquisition of the asset will be funded with borrowed capital, there will be an interest of 10% on the Rs. 75 Mn which is Rs. 7.5 Mn. Hence the interest will go up from Rs. 140 Mn to Rs. 147.5 Mn (rounded to Rs. 148 Mn)

No	Description	Formula	Rs. Mn		Scenario 1
					Impact of Capital expense
A	Revenue from operations		26,500		26,500
B	Direct Material cost		19,978		19,978
C	Employee Benefit		1,345		1,345
D	Manufacturing expense		1,836		1,836
E	Sales & Admin expense		529		529
F	Gross Margin	A-B-C-D-E	2,812		2,812
G	Depreciation		631		641
H	Margin after Depreciation	F-G	2,181		2,171
I	Interest payment		140		148
J	Profit before Tax (PBT)	H-I	2,041	7.7%	2,024
K	Tax		510		506
L	Profit after tax (PAT)	J-K	1,531		1,518
	Earnings per Share		43.99		43.61
	ROCE		37.66%		37.48%
	ROE		39.70%		39.36%

The profit (PAT) has reduced from Rs. 1531 Mn to Rs. 1518 Mn. The earnings per share dropped by Rs. 0.28 per share. The ROCE has reduced by 0.18% percentage point. The ROE has dropped by 0.34% percentage point.

Syed was upset that his initiative to reduce cost has ended up with a proposal to spend Rs. 75 Mn on capital expenditure and reduction in financial parameters, though he is convinced that the above expense is essential to ensure high availability of critical machines.

Syed looks at other options.

Several non-critical machines on the production floor were not at their best. Since they were not critical assets, the attention given was lower. Syed decided to improve their availability which is relatively easier, since they are not at their best. He discusses with the supply chain team to understand the kind of subcontracting activities that are being outsourced. By comparing the machines available with the subcontractors and the non-critical machines that are available at the company, Syed lists down 10 non-critical machines that can make some subcontracted parts, if the availability of such machines is improved. With this information, he meets Anil to sound his idea with him. Due to the friendly and supportive nature of Syed, it was not very tough for Syed to validate his idea and obtain the support of Anil on this initiative. On discussing with Anil, they could see the possibility of bringing some of the parts from outsourcing to Inhouse manufacturing, provided the machine availability is increased. The value of such items which could be brought from outsourced to in-house machining was Rs 50 Mn. This would increase the cost of tooling/consumables by about Rs 5 Mn.

With the help of Raj, Syed prepared the P&L as follows.

The Material cost was reduced by Rs. 50 Mn since the subcontracting was reduced. The manufacturing cost increased by Rs. 5 Mn due to the purchase of additional toolings.

No	Description	Formula	Rs. Mn		Scenario 2 reduction in sub contracting
A	Revenue from operations		26,500		26,500
B	Direct Material cost		19,978		19,928
C	Employee Benefit		1,345		1,345
D	Manufacturing expense		1,836		1,841
E	Sales & Admin expense		529		529
F	Gross Margin	A-B-C-D-E	2,812		2,857
G	Depreciation		631		631
H	Margin after Depreciation	F-G	2,181		2,226
I	Interest payment		140		140
J	Profit before Tax (PBT)	H-I	2,041	7.7%	2,086
K	Tax		510		522
L	Profit after tax (PAT)	J-K	1,531		1,565
	Earnings per Share		43.99		44.96
	ROCE		37.66%		38.43%
	ROE		39.70%		40.57%

Eventually, the profit increased from Rs. 1531 Mn to Rs. 1565 Mn.

The EPS increased from Rs. 43.99 to Rs. 44.96

The ROCE increased from 37.66% to Rs. 38.43%

The ROE increased from 39.70% to 40.57%

Syed was happy that by combining the above 2 initiatives he can show improvement in the financials. He was ready to be called by Vishal. However, he strongly believed that one should not rest with the first success but should explore further potential. Hence, he decided to explore more potential.

He reviewed with his team the list of maintenance spare parts that are in the inventory. Since ABC Limited had a large production floor, a high level of maintenance spare parts inventory was maintained. Some of the spare parts were not used for many years. However, he knows that most of them are emergency spares and it was too risky for him to dispose of such spare parts. His team identified some obsolete spare parts which they decided to discard. Since these are old spare parts they were already written off in the previous years and do not have any impact on the current year's financial statement of the company. This exercise has not yielded any impact on the financials however sprucing up the inventory and making it clean is always good.

How he could reduce the expenses for the company further? This question constantly haunted Syed. He discussed with some of his contacts outside the company and identified new areas for cost reduction. He understood that some companies are moving to renewable energy which costs less than the conventional energy source. He talked to companies that are in renewable energy such as Solar and Windmills. He understands that ABC Limited can buy renewable energy from such producers which can be offset against the purchase from the government energy source.

Let's not get into the details of this work. Let's conclude that Syed was able to save some energy costs through this method. In addition to this Syed worked on alternatives to the various consumables used in the Shop Floor for regular running and maintenance of the machines. He could see some potential in these areas too. With this cost reduction initiative, he and his team could see a potential saving of about Rs. 65 Mn in the current year.

As an exercise, you may kindly prepare a P&L to see the impact of the reduction of Rs. 65 Mn on the manufacturing expense.

With this calculation on hand, Syed was ready to meet Vishal. Needless to mention Syed had a very good meeting with Vishal as he was fully prepared. Vishal was thoroughly impressed by Syed's preparedness and his out-of-the-box thinking.

Snippet – 10

India contributed to modern financial accounting through innovative ideas and culturally influenced practices:

o *Establishment of the **Institute of Cost Accountants of India (ICMAI)** in 1944 to focus on cost management, a pioneer among developing nations.*
o *India's banking and financial sector reforms post-1991 introduced **Non-Performing Asset (NPA)** recognition and capital adequacy norms.*
o *These became benchmarks for emerging markets.*
o *India has led in transitioning to **digital accounting systems**, especially after the introduction of the **Goods and Services Tax (GST)**, which required unified digital compliance.*
o *Indian Chartered Accountants and finance professionals are globally recognized for their expertise, significantly influencing global accounting standards.*

Brain GYM – V

1. Prepare a P&L to see the impact of the reduction of Rs. 65 Mn on the manufacturing expense referred to in the previous page.
2. Prepare a P&L by combining the Scenario 1 & 2 referred to in the above chapter.

CHAPTER TEN

QUALITY ASSURANCE

"The guardian of excellence, ensuring every product reflects the promise of your brand."

Quality of products and services is the foundation for any business. Quality may not be an area to look for cost reduction. However, there are areas where the Quality function could consider reducing cost.

The areas in which a quality department could contribute to expense reduction are

- Reduction in the cost of warranty or post-sale expenses
- Avoiding production stoppage due to a wrong part cleared by the Quality team.
- Manpower reduction in the quality function, etc.

The reduction in the warranty expense has a double effect. It increases the profit to the extent of a reduction in the warranty expense and it increases the reputation of the product as there are fewer failures.

The warranty expense reduction as an exercise can be spearheaded by the quality function by analyzing the various failures in the field and arriving at solutions such as design modification, process modification, improved inspection, etc.

By improving the inspection process the possibility of a wrong component getting approved by the quality could be eliminated or brought to a negligible level thus ensuring that there is no stoppage in the line.

By introducing self-certified vendors, the manpower cost in quality function may be reduced. However, developing a self-certified vendor is not an easy task. Some companies make the mistake of declaring a vendor as self-certified based on their acceptance level of previous supplies. If a vendor supplies components without rejection for the past 10 occasions or more in one year they may get certified as a self-certified vendor. But more important than this is to understand whether the vendor has a process control that delivers 100% accepted components every time. If the process is not robust and not monitored continuously, errors may creep in at any time.

With modern technology, there are several opportunities for eliminating conventional inspection through digital technology. Many companies use image processing to inspect a component. 3D scanning is another technology that could reduce or eliminate inspection. In many cases, this improves the accuracy level of the inspection.

Through such initiatives, manpower costs could be reduced. However, in most industries, the manpower cost of quality people is insignificant to the total cost. Hence, I am not preparing a table to indicate the impact of the manpower reduction.

I would like to showcase just one table considering the reduction in the warranty costs which is normally indicated as a provision on the books of accounts. It is represented as a percentage on the sale value. For our understanding let's assume the current warranty cost for the company is 0.9% and the quality function takes a target to reduce it to 0.75%, which is a reduction of 0.15% on the sale value.

Normally the cost of warranty is added to the material cost or it may be added to the sales and distribution costs. In our example, I'm considering it in the material cost.

The material cost shown in the table is Rs. 19978 Mn.

The reduction in warranty cost by 0.15% on Rs. 26500 is Rs. 40 Mn. So, the material cost will reduce from Rs. 19978 Mn to Rs. 19938 Mn.

No	Description	Formula	Rs. Mn		Scenario 1 Impact of warranty cost reduction
A	revenue from operations		26,500		26,500
B	Direct Material cost		19,978		19,938
C	Employee Benefit		1,345		1,345
D	Manufacturing expense		1,836		1,836
E	Sales & Admin expense		529		529
F	Gross Margin	A-B-C-D-E	2,812		2,852
G	Depreciation		631		631
H	Margin after Depreciation	F-G	2,181		2,221
I	Interest payment		140		140
J	Profit before Tax (PBT)	H-I	2,041	7.7%	2,081
K	Tax		510		520
L	Profit after tax (PAT)	J-K	1,531		1,561
	Earnings per Share		43.99		44.84
	ROCE		37.66%		38.34%
	ROE		39.70%		40.47%

This results in an increase of Rs 40 Mn on the PBT.

The earnings per share increased from Rs. 43.99 to Rs. 44.84.

The ROCE increased from 37.66% to 38.34%

The ROE increased from 39.70% to 40.47%.

Understanding the importance of quality and to ensure that the quality team does not focus on cost reduction, Vishal decided not to invite Giridhar, head of quality for a discussion on cost reduction. However, Giridhar is a person who always aligns with the company's initiative very swiftly. Hence, he voluntarily meets Vishal to share his initiative. Vishal appreciated Giridhar. They engaged in an in-depth discussion on how to further improve quality levels and instill a quality-driven mindset in every employee.

CHAPTER ELEVEN

ENGINEERING

"Crafting solutions that transform possibilities into practical innovations."

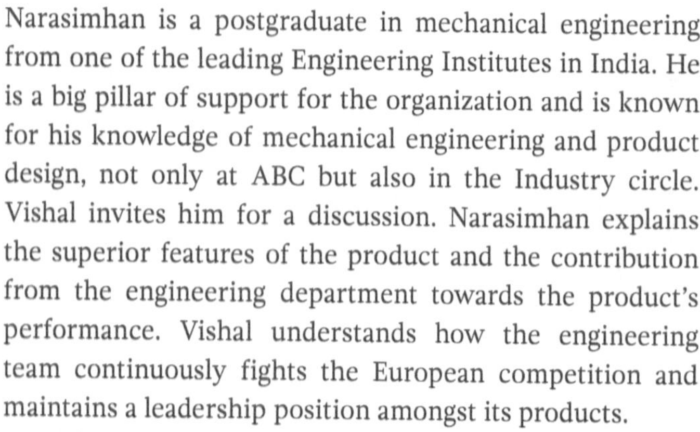

Narasimhan is a postgraduate in mechanical engineering from one of the leading Engineering Institutes in India. He is a big pillar of support for the organization and is known for his knowledge of mechanical engineering and product design, not only at ABC but also in the Industry circle. Vishal invites him for a discussion. Narasimhan explains the superior features of the product and the contribution from the engineering department towards the product's performance. Vishal understands how the engineering team continuously fights the European competition and maintains a leadership position amongst its products.

Vishal feels that he should not dilute the focus of the engineering team from its core job of product innovation. Hence, he suggests forming a small team of two to three engineers to work on cost reduction. Vishal strongly believes that the cost of the product is frozen at the time of designing it. The purchase and the manufacturing team have a limited role in controlling this cost.

Vishal and Narasimhan decided to meet after 2 weeks along with the new team with whom they could brainstorm avenues for cost reduction.

After 2 weeks Narasimhan introduces 2 of his young engineers Amit and Savithri as a chosen one for this work. As a team, they discussed various avenues for cost reduction, including,

- Evaluation of major components for its functionality. Whether the material of construction, thickness, etc are optimised or is there a scope for improvement.
- As 3D printing is gaining acceptance in the manufacturing sector Amit and Savitri agree to review critical assemblies which could be made as a single 3D printed component instead of multiple manufactured components
- Possibilities of using Castings instead of complicated fabrication components. Similarly, simple castings may be replaced with fabrication.

With all these inputs engineering team works meticulously and evolves a plan for a potential savings of 1.5% on the material cost.

Readers, the table below is very similar to the one presented in the supply chain chapter except that the reduction considered here is 1.5% whereas in the supply chain chapter, it was at 1%.

As you can see from the table

The PBT has increased from Rs. 2041 Mn to Rs. 2340.7 Mn.

The EPS has gone up from Rs. 43.99 to Rs. 50.45

The ROCE has increased from 37.66% to 42.83%

The ROE increased from 39.70% to 45.53%

No.	Description	Formula	Rs. Mn		Scenario 1 Material Cost reduction
A	Revenue from operations		26,500.0		26,500.0
B	Direct Material cost		19,978.0		19,678.3
C	Employee Benefit		1,345.0		1,345.0
D	Manufacturing expense		1,836.0		1,836.0
E	Sales & Admin expense		529.0		529.0
F	Gross Margin	A-B-C-D-E	2,812.0		3,111.7
G	Depreciation		631.0		631.0
H	Margin after Depreciation	F-G	2,181.0		2,480.7
I	Interest payment		140.0		140.0
J	Profit before Tax	H-I	2,041.0		2,340.7
K	Tax		510.3		585.2
L	Profit after tax	J-K	1,530.8	6%	1,755.5
	Earnings per Share		43.99		50.45
	ROCE		37.66%		42.83%
	ROE		39.70%		45.53%

The other area where Engineering could play a significant role is in reducing the warranty cost by improving the design. This was discussed in the Quality function area too.

Engineering can also enhance the value of the product through the increase in features or increasing the life of the wear parts and reducing the consumption of consumables, etc. This will help in getting a higher price from the market thus increasing the profit for the company. This was discussed in the marketing Chapter and hence I am not repeating the same here.

Brain GYM – VI

1. The Engineering department makes certain improvements in the product (without an increase in the cost of the product) thus increasing the intrinsic value of the product. Pl prepare a P&L considering the possibility of an increase in selling price by 1% from the current level without an increase in any other expenses.

CHAPTER TWELVE

SOME MORE LEARNING

Return on Investment

Enthused by the success, the Production Head Mr. Anil Sharma wanted to explore whether they could add some more machines and reduce the subcontracting further. Anil identified a few machines to add to his shop floor. The cost of which including the installation commissioning would come to Rs 100 Mn. He discussed with the purchasing team to identify the components that could be manufactured in-house and the potential cash flow reduction due to reduced sub-contracting. He identified that Rs. 20 Mn worth of subcontracting can be reduced by manufacturing these components using these new machines. He was not sure whether this would be accepted by the management. He took the help of the finance head to understand how this can be presented. The very basic model of the cash flow was prepared by Raj considering the reduction in subcontracting.

Raj asked what are the other expenses related to the operations of this machine. Anil replied, "I need to increase the manpower and incur cost for running the machine (cost of electricity and consumables). Based on this basic information Raj prepared the following table.

When we build a table for future income and expense, it is normal not to consider inflation on both sides; income & expense. This makes the table simple to analyse. All tables presented in the book do not consider inflation.

Particulars	Yr1	Yr2	Yr3	Yr4	Yr5	Yr6	Yr7	Yr8	Yr9	Yr10
sub-contracting saved	20.00	20.00	20.00	20.00	20.00	20.00	20.00	20.00	20.00	20.00
expenses for manpower	1.44	1.44	1.44	1.44	1.44	1.44	1.44	1.44	1.44	1.44
Expenses for power and consumables	1.54	1.54	1.54	1.54	1.54	1.54	1.54	1.54	1.54	1.54
Net cashflow	17.02	17.02	17.02	17.02	17.02	17.02	17.02	17.02	17.02	17.02

Anil was thrilled to see this result as you could see a saving of Rs. 17 Mn year on year. The CFO cautioned, "Please wait, we have to factor non-cash related expenses. When we add the plant and machinery to our assets, we should consider depreciation for these machines. Let's put our standard policy for depreciation i.e. 10 years. If we follow a very simple linear 10-year depreciation, each year, depreciation will be Rs. 10 Mn. We need to remove this from the Rs. 17 Mn. The result would be Rs. 7 Mn year on year."

Particulars	Yr1	Yr2	Yr3	Yr4	Yr5	Yr6	Yr7	Yr8	Yr9	Yr10
sub-contracting saved	20.00	20.00	20.00	20.00	20.00	20.00	20.00	20.00	20.00	20.00
expenses for manpower	1.44	1.44	1.44	1.44	1.44	1.44	1.44	1.44	1.44	1.44
Expenses for power and consumables	1.54	1.54	1.54	1.54	1.54	1.54	1.54	1.54	1.54	1.54
Net cashflow	17.02	17.02	17.02	17.02	17.02	17.02	17.02	17.02	17.02	17.02
Non Cash expense - depreciation	10.00	10.00	10.00	10.00	10.00	10.00	10.00	10.00	10.00	10.00
Net return expected from this investment	7.02	7.02	7.02	7.02	7.02	7.02	7.02	7.02	7.02	7.02

Anil felt a bit disappointed. He asked Raj, what do you think? Raj replied, "If you are purely looking at the numbers, Rs 7 Mn on an investment of Rs. 100 Mn is just about 7% per annum. As you can see our company is currently having more than 30% as a return on capital employed. This is lower than the average return on capital employed and hence will pull down our ROCE." Raj suggested, "Please discuss this with Vishal to see whether it makes a business proposal or not. If avoiding dependence on outside resources is considered very strategic, then he may accept. I am not competent to decide on this and I suggest you discuss with Vishal." Raj said.

Provision/Write-Off

It is quite normal that a company buys certain spare parts for maintaining the machines. Some of the parts may not be used for several years. They may become obsolete. For example, seals and rubber parts have a shelf life, beyond which they need to be scraped. Some of the electronic parts may become redundant due to changes in technology or the requirement of upgrading the machines with the latest technology. Hence, it's common that the company would end up with inventory that is not useful or that cannot be sold in the market to monetize it. Hence the companies establish a policy for making provisions in the financial statement so that their financial statements reflect a more realistic picture. (Provision is a heading under which the company reserves a certain amount for an expense that has not been incurred but is likely to be incurred at any time.)

For example, this company has an inventory of Rs. 1236 Mn. This inventory could have been purchased for carrying out their regular orders received from customers, items required for maintenance, consumable items, tools, etcetera. At the end of the year, the company analyses the inventory of each group.

The company takes the aging report of such inventory to identify items that have not been consumed for 2 to 3 years. This inventory can potentially become unusable in the future. Hence as a prudent accounting principle, the company writes a policy which could be as follows.

If an item is not used for 2 years, 50% of its value should be reduced from the inventory value.

If an item is not used for 3 years, 100% of its value should be reduced from the inventory value.

For eg.

Let us assume the inventory at the end of the year was Rs. 1400 Mn.

Out of this Rs. 272 Mn was not used for 2 years and Rs. 100 Mn was not used for 3 years. Let us call these items as Slowing moving inventory and Non-moving inventory respectively. The company may have a policy to write off 100% value of non-moving inventory and 50% of the slow-moving inventory as an expense in the financials.

The total inventory – Rs. 1400 Mn

Provision for slow-moving inventory

Rs. 50% of Rs. 272 Mn – Rs. 136 Mn

Provision for Non-moving inventory

100% of Rs. 100 Mn – Rs. 100 Mn.

So the total provision is - Rs. 236 Mn.

This would sound insane to write off Rs. 236 Mn. Please remember that this company has been in operation for several years. Hence, they would have done a similar exercise the previous year and would have written off some amount, let's say it was Rs. 200 Mn. For the current year only the difference of Rs. 236 Mn – Rs. 200 MN will be written off.

If the company can reduce it's non-moving and slow-moving by finding avenues to use it for creating revenue, then the provision may turn out to be positive. For example, let's say the current year provision is Rs. 150 Mn instead of Rs. 236 Mn. The difference of Rs. 236 Mn and Rs. 150 Mn, that is Rs. 86 Mn will add to the profit.

CHAPTER THIRTEEN

CONCLUSION

"Every end is a new beginning—lead with confidence and clarity."

As we reach the end of this book, I hope it has given you the knowledge and confidence to approach finance with a fresh perspective. From understanding the basics of business finance to exploring how companies measure success, this journey has been about making business finance simple to understand and apply.

Remember, learning is a lifelong journey. Every new challenge is an opportunity to grow and apply what you've learned. Whether you're managing your finances or contributing to a business, knowing how to connect numbers with action will always set you apart.

I encourage you to take these lessons forward and use them to make a difference—in your work, your decisions, and your life. The future will be bright and predictable to those who understand the numbers and use them wisely.

Before we conclude this book, I would like to spend a few minutes on Personal Finance. Unless we manage ourselves properly there is no way we can manage the business properly. I have added a few pages to kindle your thoughts on personal finance management.

The Personal Pillar

CHAPTER FOURTEEN

PERSONAL FINANCE

"Master your money, and you'll master your future"

It is very important that every individual has financial prudence for managing their life properly by ensuring that they do not end up in a financial trap. I strongly believe that many of the practices that are being followed in a company / Corporate are applicable to the personal life as well.

For example, in factories, we follow preventive maintenance and condition-based maintenance of machines. We also conduct risk assessments for the business. When it comes to our personal lives, we do not take care of our health through preventive maintenance, like exercise, yoga, meditation, etcetera. Our body is probably the most complicated equipment in this world, It has a self-healing capability, provided we allow it to do its work. Needless to mention most of us hardly pay any attention to it.

Similarly, risk assessment of any business is very vital and should be conducted at a regular interval. Similarly, the risk assessment for our lives is also important. Some people take huge risks without taking adequate care for any unfavourable outcome.

Firstly, I consider our balance sheet as one of the most important criteria for us to evaluate.

Assets refer to the movable and immovable properties that we may possess. Liabilities refer to the loans that we might have taken for various purposes like education, jewel purchases, housing loans, appliance purchases, etc. A typical Balance Sheet is as follows.

Balance sheet	Rs. Mn
Asset	
House	10
Other Properties (Land)	5
Shares (Stocks)	2
FD and cash	1
Jewel	1
Car	1
	20
Liability	
Housing loan	7
Jewel loan	1
Any other loan (education)	1
	9

In the case of the balance sheet of a company, it is essential to balance the Assets and the Liabilities. However, for personal finance, I feel it is sufficient if we know our current status, i.e. whether our assets are more than our liabilities or otherwise.

This would give us a feeling of whether we are in a comfort zone or we are in a risk zone. If the liability is much higher than the asset, then we know we need to do something to address this issue. It could be that we need to plan for a few years to see how we will reduce the Liabilities to bring it below the Assets level.

Another very important category of financial control in our personal life will be cash flow management. This is where some of the people fail. They commit expenses without ensuring the inflow of money.

Let me share with you a typical cash flow working that could serve as an example for you to prepare your cash flow statement.

You may observe from the cash flow table that the inflow represents the salary income or business income, rental income, interest income, or at times, the loan that we may take for various purposes. The outflow represents the monthly household expenses, your investments, purchase of assets, school fees, marriage expenses etcetera. The last line represents the net cash flow, which indicates whether you have enough cash during that particular year to handle the expenses. If the number falls in negative it means you don't have enough cash. If the number is positive it means that you have cash which you may consider investing or saving for meeting the negative expenses in subsequent years.

Particulars	Rs. In Mn	Yr1	Yr2	Yr3	Yr4	Yr5	Yr6	Yr7	Yr8	Yr9	Yr10	Yr11	Yr12	Yr13	Yr14	Yr15
Inflow																
Salary Income after tax		5.00	5.25	5.51	5.79	6.08	6.38	6.70	7.04	7.39	7.76	8.14	8.55	8.98	9.43	9.90
Other income – rental, FD		0.10	0.10	0.10	0.10	0.10	0.10	0.10	0.20	0.20	0.20	0.20	0.20	0.20	0.20	0.20
Loan		0.00	0.00	0.00	7.00	0.00	0.00	0.00	0.00	0.00	0.00	0.00	0.00	0.00	0.00	0.00
		5.10	**5.35**	**5.61**	**12.89**	**6.18**	**6.48**	**6.80**	**7.24**	**7.59**	**7.96**	**8.34**	**8.75**	**9.18**	**9.63**	**10.10**
Outflow																
Monthly house hold expense		3.60	3.78	3.97	4.17	4.38	4.59	4.82	5.07	5.32	5.58	5.86	6.16	6.47	6.79	7.13
investment in SIP, Jewels, shares		0.20	0.22	0.24	0.27	0.29	0.32	0.35	0.39	0.43	0.47	0.52	0.57	0.63	0.69	0.76
Asset purchase					10.00											
loan repayment		0.00	0.00	0.00	0.00	0.70	0.70	0.70	0.70	0.70	0.70	0.70	0.70	0.70	0.70	0.70
Children school fees		0.20	0.21	0.22	0.23	0.24	0.26	0.27	0.28	0.30	0.31	0.33	0.34	0.36	0.38	0.40
Children college admission		0.00	0.00	0.00	0.00	0.00	0.00	0.00	0.00	0.00	0.00	0.00	1.00	1.00	1.00	1.00
Children marriage		0.00	0.00	0.00	0.00	0.00	0.00	0.00	0.00	0.00	0.00	0.00	0.00	0.00	0.00	0.00
		4.00	**4.21**	**4.43**	**14.67**	**5.61**	**5.87**	**6.15**	**6.44**	**6.74**	**7.07**	**7.41**	**8.77**	**9.15**	**9.56**	**9.98**
Net cashflow		**1.10**	**1.14**	**1.18**	**-1.78**	**0.57**	**0.61**	**0.65**	**0.80**	**0.84**	**0.89**	**0.94**	**-0.02**	**0.03**	**0.07**	**0.12**

This is just an indicative table you may build something that is more specific to your application and you may even make it on a monthly basis if you would like to have a very close control of the cash flow.

I fondly recall an incident in my life. 10 years ago I was planning to construct a house in Chennai by selling some shares and also taking a loan from the bank. I approached an architect and a builder. I signed a contract with each of them for design and building of the house. I also approached the bankers for loan. We started the work of soil testing, water testing, surveying the land, design for the house, etc. When this was going on, my wife asked me a very pertinent question, "I'm happy that you're building a house but do you realize that you have two major expenses coming up in the next few years? One, higher studies for our son and another is the marriage for our daughter. Have you earmarked funds for this?' I was very angry with her that she raised this question now, after I had already spent a few lakhs of rupees on this project. Later I realized the importance of that question. I drew up my cash flow statement for the next 5 to 6 years and found that I'm not carrying enough money to handle those major expenses. Eventually I cancelled the housing project despite having spent few lakhs on it. Had I not done this I would have certainly got into financial trap having spent the huge money on the House and struggled to meet the other essential expenses.

AASK

Please do not stop with Acquiring knowledge. Please apply
it and also share it.

I believe in Aask
(Acquire, Apply, and Share Knowledge).

Let's make the world more knowledgeable.

ANSWERS

Brain GYM -I

1. Amswer

Description	Formula	Rs. Mn	Rs. Mn
Revenue from sale of 1.5 Mn pens			30.00
Other Income			0.30
Interest from Bank Deposit of free cash		0.01	
Duty draw back from customs	1% of Rs. 15 Mn	0.15	
Sale of duty free licence scrip @ 1% of exports sold for 5% discount	1% of Rs. 15 Mn * 0.95	0.1425	
Sale of assets (car)			
Total Revenue			30.30
	0		
Cost of Raw material		15.00	
Cost of Sub Contracting		4.50	
Cost of Direct labour		3.00	
Total Direct Cost			22.50
	0		
Administrative, Sales and Distribution expenses			1.10
Gross Margin	A-B-C		6.70
Depreciation			3.50
Margin after Depreciation	D-E		3.20
Interest payment			0.25
Profit before Tax (after Interest payment)	F-G		2.95
Tax			0.74
Profit after tax	H-I		2.21

2. Profit before tax = 9.73%, Return on Investment = 2.95/70.7 = 4.2%

Brain GYM – II

1. Answer for the ROCE and ROE for 3 scenarios

No.	Description	Formula	Rs. Mn		Scenario 1	Scenario 2	Scenario 3
					Material Cost reduction	credit terms with Vendors	reduction in Inventory
A	Revenue from operations		26,500		26,500.0	26,500.0	26,500.0
B	Direct Material cost		19,978		19,778.2	19,978.0	19,978.0
C	Employee Benefit		1,345		1,345.0	1,345.0	1,345.0
D	Manufacturing expense		1,836		1,836.0	1,836.0	1,836.0
E	Sales & Admin expense		529		529.0	529.0	529.0
F	Gross Margin	A-B-C-D-E	2,812		3,011.8	2,812.0	2,812.0
G	Depreciation		631		631.0	631.0	631.0
H	Margin after Depreciation	F-G	2,181		2,380.8	2,181.0	2,181.0
I	Interest payment		140		140.0	129.1	127.6
J	Profit before Tax (after Interest payment)	H-I	2,041		2,240.8	2,051.9	2,053.4
K	Tax		510	6%	560.2	513.0	513.3
L	Profit after tax	J-K	1,531		1,680.6	1,539.0	1,540.0
	Earnings per Share		43.99		48.29	44.22	44.25
	ROCE		37.66%		41.10%	37.66%	37.66%
	ROE		39.70%		43.58%	39.91%	39.94%

2. Effect of all the 3 scenarios when implemented together

No.	Description	Formula	Rs. Mn		All 3 scenarios
A	Revenue from operations		26,500		26,500.0
B	Direct Material cost		19,978		19,778.2
C	Employee Benefit		1,345		1,345.0
D	Manufacturing expense		1,836		1,836.0
E	Sales & Admin expense		529		529.0
F	Gross Margin	A-B-C-D-E	2,812		3,011.8
G	Depreciation		631		631.0
H	Margin after Depreciation	F-G	2,181		2,380.8
I	Interest payment		140		116.7
J	Profit before Tax (after Interest payment)	H-I	2,041		2,264.1
K	Tax		510		566.0
L	Profit after tax	J-K	1,531		1,698.1
	Earnings per Share		43.99		48.79
	ROCE		37.66%		41.10%
	ROE		39.70%		44.04%

Brain GYM – III

1. Answer

Brain GYM								
Sales segmentation	Sales Rs. Mn (A)	DMC (B)	Direct MFG Cost (C)	Total cost (D= B+C)	Contribution % from the above table	Contribution Rs. Mn (sales * Contribution %)		Increase/ Decrease in Sale
Product A	12000	9240	840	10080	16.0%	1920		
Product B	5640	4568	338.4	4907	13.0%	733		-6%
Product C	5000	3600	250	3850	23.0%	1150		
Product D	3675	2392	183.75	2576	29.9%	1099		5%
	26315	19800	1612	21412		4903		

No.	Description	Formula	Rs. Mn		Brain GYM 1
A	Revenue from operations		26,500		26,315
B	Direct Material cost		19,978		19,800
C	Employee Benefit		1,345		1,345
D	Manufacturing expense		1,836		1,836
E	Sales & Admin expense		529		529
F	Gross Margin	A-B-C-D-E	2,812		2,805
G	Depreciation		631		631
H	Margin after Depreciation	F-G	2,181		2,174
I	Interest payment		140		140
J	Profit before Tax	H-I	2,041		2,034
K	Tax		510		508
L	Profit after tax	J-K	1,531	5.8%	1,525
	Earnings per Share		43.99		43.83
	ROCE		37.66%		37.53%
	ROE		39.70%		39.56%

2. Answer

Brain GYM - 2

Sales segmentation	Sales Rs. Mn (A)	DMC (B)	Direct MFG Cost (C)	Total cost (D= B+C)	Contribution % from the above table	Contribution Rs. Mn (sales * Contribution %)		Price increase
Product A	12060	9240	840	10080	16.4%	1980		0.5%
Product B	6060	4860	360	5220	13.9%	840		1.0%
Product C	4975	3600	250	3850	22.6%	1125		-0.5%
Product D	3500	2278	175	2453	29.9%	1047		0.0%
	26595	19978	1625	21603		4992		

No.	Description	Formula	Rs. Mn		Brain GYM 2
A	Revenue from operations		26,500		26,595
B	Direct Material cost		19,978	######	19,978
C	Employee Benefit		1,345		1,345
D	Manufacturing expense		1,836	6.9%	1,836
E	Sales & Admin expense		529	2.0%	529
F	Gross Margin	A-B-C-D-E	2,812		2,907
G	Depreciation		631		631
H	Margin after Depreciation	F-G	2,181		2,276
I	Interest payment		140		140
J	Profit before Tax	H-I	2,041		2,136
K	Tax		510		534
L	Profit after tax	J-K	1,531	5.8%	1,602
	Earnings per Share		43.99		46.03
	ROCE		37.66%		39.30%
	ROE		39.70%		41.55%

Brain GYM – IV

1. Answer

Description	Formula	Rs. Mn		Brain GYM 1
Revenue from operations		26,500		26,500
Direct Material cost		19,978		19,628
Employee Benefit		1,345		1,350
Manufacturing expense		1,836		1,911
Sales & Admin expense		529		529
Gross Margin	A-B-C-D-E	2,812		3,082
Depreciation		631		631
Margin after Depreciation	F-G	2,181		2,451
Interest payment		140		140
Profit before Tax (PBT)	H-I	2,041	7.7%	2,311
Tax		510		578
Profit after tax (PAT)	J-K	1,531		1,733
Earnings per Share		43.99		49.81
ROCE		37.66%		42.32%
ROE		39.70%		44.95%

2. Answer

Balance Sheet				Brain GYM
Description	Rs. Mn	Rs. Mn		2
Equity Share capital		348.0		348.0
Reserves and Surplus		3,508.0		3,334.0
Total shareholders funds	a+b	3,856.0		3,682.0
Long term borrowings		1,211.0		1,211.0
Other liabilities and long term provisions		725.0		725.0
Total non current liabilities	c+d	1,936.0		1,936.0
Short term borrowings		1,033.0		1,033.0
Trade payables		4,130.0		4,130.0
Other current liabilities and provision		845.0		845.0
Total current liabilities	e+f+g	6,008.0		6,008.0
Grand total of liabilities	**A+B+C**	**11,800.0**		11,626.0
Assets				
Tangible assets		6,260.0		6,260.0
Intangible asset		688.0		688.0
Capital WIP		574.0		574.0
Other financial assets		611.0		611.0
Total non current asset	h+i+j+k	8,133.0		8,133.0
Current investments		191.0		191.0
Inventories		1,236.0		1,236.0
Trade receivables		955.0		955.0
Cash and cash equivalents		242.0		68.0
Other current assets		1,043.0		1,043.0
Total current assets	m+n+o+p+q	3,667.0		3,493.0
Grand total of the asset	D+E	11,800.0		11,626.0
Earnings per Share				43.99
ROCE				38.82%
ROE				41.57%

Brain GYM – V

1. Answer

No	Description	Formula	Rs. Mn		Brain GYM reduction in Mfg expense
A	Revenue from operations		26,500		26,500
B	Direct Material cost		19,978		19,978
C	Employee Benefit		1,345		1,345
D	Manufacturing expense		1,836		1,771
E	Sales & Admin expense		529		529
F	Gross Margin	A-B-C-D-E	2,812		2,877
G	Depreciation		631		631
H	Margin after Depreciation	F-G	2,181		2,246
I	Interest payment		140		140
J	Profit before Tax (PBT)	H-I	2,041	7.7%	2,106
K	Tax		510		527
L	Profit after tax (PAT)	J-K	1,531		1,580
	Earnings per Share		43.99		45.39
	ROCE		37.66%		38.78%
	ROE		39.70%		40.96%

2. Answer

No	Description	Formula	Rs. Mn	Scenario 1 Impact of Capital expense	Scenario 2 reduction in sub contracting	Scenario 1+2 after considering the impact of capital expense
A	Revenue from operations		26,500	26,500	26,500	26,500
B	Direct Material cost		19,978	19,978	19,928	19,928
C	Employee Benefit		1,345	1,345	1,345	1,345
D	Manufacturing expense		1,836	1,836	1,841	1,841
E	Sales & Admin expense		529	529	529	529
F	Gross Margin	A-B-C-D-E	2,812	2,812	2,857	2,857
G	Depreciation		631	641	631	641
H	Margin after Depreciation	F-G	2,181	2,171	2,226	2,216
I	Interest payment		140	148	140	148
J	Profit before Tax (PBT)	H-I	2,041	2,024	2,086	2,069
K	Tax		510	506	522	517
L	Profit after tax (PAT)	J-K	1,531	1,518	1,565	1,551
	Earnings per Share		43.99	43.61	44.96	44.58
	ROCE		37.66%	37.48%	38.43%	37.77%
	ROE		39.70%	39.36%	40.57%	40.23%

Brain GYM – VI

1. Answer

No.	Description	Formula	Rs. Mn		Brain GYM Increase in Selling Price
A	Revenue from operations		26,500.0		26,765.0
B	Direct Material cost		19,978.0		19,978.0
C	Employee Benefit		1,345.0		1,345.0
D	Manufacturing expense		1,836.0		1,836.0
E	Sales & Admin expense		529.0		529.0
F	Gross Margin	A-B-C-D-E	2,812.0		3,077.0
G	Depreciation		631.0		631.0
H	Margin after Depreciation	F-G	2,181.0		2,446.0
I	Interest payment		140.0		140.0
J	Profit before Tax	H-I	2,041.0		2,306.0
K	Tax		510.3		576.5
L	Profit after tax	J-K	1,530.8	[illegible]	1,729.5
	Earnings per Share		43.99		49.70
	ROCE		37.66%		42.23%
	ROE		39.70%		44.85%

About The Author

Arul Shanmugavelu is an engineer who furthered his education with a management degree. After working for a short period at HCL Limited, Dehradun and General Optics (Asia) Limited, Pondicherry he joined Larsen & Toubro Limited (L&T). In L&T, he worked for 30 years, in various functional areas such as purchase, import and export logistics, domestic & international marketing, customer service, and product development. During this period he traveled to many countries and dealt with people from various cultures. In 2014, he was appointed as the chief executive of one of the subsidiaries of L&T. Later this unit was purchased by Kobe Steel, Ltd, Japan, and named Kobelco Industrial Machinery India Private Limited. At the time of publishing this book, he was serving as the Country Head at Kobelco Industrial Machinery India Private Limited.

Arul is passionate about sharing his knowledge with others. He conducts training programs on Effective Living, Fun with Finance, and Goal Setting. He is also actively involved in social service.

He lives in Chennai with his wife Sathya. Their daughter and son-in-law are practicing Doctors in Chennai and their son is doing his Doctorate in Robotics in the US.

His first & second books on career growth "French Fries" & "Daily Bytes" were well appreciated by the readers with a 5-star rating on Amazon.

He can be contacted at arulshanmugavelu@yahoo.com.

www.ingramcontent.com/pod-product-compliance
Lightning Source LLC
Chambersburg PA
CBHW021543150726
47990CB00006B/2375